Vocabulary WORKS

Level **B**

Dr. Marjorie Merwin King   **Dr. Alvin Granowsky**

ISBN: 0-8136-1722-7
Printed in the United States of America
18 19 20   V088   13 12 11

Modern Curriculum Press
Pearson Learning Group

1-800-321-3106
www.pearsonlearning.com

TABLE OF CONTENTS

FISH DANCE
ON THE BEACH

Can fish **dance**? The grunion can. Once a year, these fish come out of the **sea**. They come onto the **beach** and **lay** their eggs.

First the fish find a spot in the sand. Then they stand on their **tails** and jump around. They look like they are dancing. But they are really digging **holes** for their eggs. As the holes get **deeper**, the fish sink into the sand. Now they can lay their eggs.

When they are done, the fish **wiggle** out of the holes. They go back to their sea homes. They need rest after a long night of dancing.

LATEST DETAILS ON DANCING FISH

What does this dancing fish do on the beach?

Check the best answer.

- ☐ It takes dancing lessons.
- ☐ It lays its eggs.
- ☐ It eats eggs.
- ☐ It rests.

ALPHABET KEEPS WORDS IN LINE

Print the New Words on the lines in ABC order.

👉 Look at the first letter of each New Word. When the first letters are the same, look at the second letters.

d<u>a</u>te comes before **d<u>e</u>nt**

NEW WORDS			
dance	sea	holes	lay
beach	tails	deeper	wiggle

1. _____

2. _____

3. _____

4. _____

5. _____

6. _____

7. _____

8. _____

WORDS AND MEANINGS TOGETHER AGAIN

Use a New Word to finish each meaning. Fill in the word shapes.

1. To put out eggs is to ⬜⬜⬜ .

2. "Down more and more" means ⬜⬜⬜⬜⬜⬜ .

3. To go back and forth is to ⬜⬜⬜⬜⬜⬜ .

4. The sandy edge of a lake is a ⬜⬜⬜⬜⬜ .

5. Things you can dig in the ground are ⬜⬜⬜⬜⬜ .

6. A large body of salt water is a ⬜⬜⬜ .

7. The parts on the ends of animals are ⬜⬜⬜⬜⬜ .

8. To move to music is to ⬜⬜⬜⬜⬜ .

TRUE OR FALSE?

The coelacanth is a fish scientists thought had died off long ago. Then, in the 1930s, they found a living one.

Answer: True

4

INCOMPLETE SENTENCES FOUND IN BOOK
MISSING WORDS MUST BE FOUND!

*Circle the word that best completes each sentence.
Then print the answers on the lines.*

1. John played in the sand on the _____ .

   deeper   peach   beach

2. He dug _____ in the sand.

   holes   halls   pails

3. Then he dug _____ into the sand.

   lay   deeper   dance

4. After a time, the _____ came in and
   washed over the hole.

   sea   see   deeper

5. Some hens are red with big black _____ .

   sea   tails   beaches

6. It is fun to _____ as the band plays.

   done   deeper   dance

7. The teacher told us not to _____ in
   our seats.

   fish   beach   wiggle

8. The turtle dug a hole to _____ its eggs.

   say   lay   pay

Fishy Facts

- At high tide, grunion ride the waves and surf to the beach. They do their dance and lay their eggs. Two weeks later, their eggs hatch, and the little surfers return to the sea.

- Contrary to popular belief, fish make noises. They groan, squeal, squawk, and bark. In fact, recordings of the underwater world sometimes sound like a barnyard gone bonkers!

WORDS JOIN TOGETHER TO FORM NEW GROUPS

👉 Some words go together in groups. **Apples**, **pears**, and **grapes** go together because they are all <u>fruit</u>.

Each New Word underlined below helps to describe a group. Circle the three words that belong in each group.

1. things at the <u>beach</u>

   sand
   shells
   lamps
   water

2. things that can <u>wiggle</u>

   snake
   pen
   worm
   tooth

3. things in the <u>sea</u>

   fish
   seaweed
   pony
   ships

TREASURE MAP MYSTERY EXPLAINED

📝 Look at this picture. The children have found a map. The map shows a box full of gold. That box was buried in the sand. Think of a story about the picture.

These questions will help you get started:

- How did the children get the map?
- What will they do to get to the buried treasure?
- Will they find gold in the box?

Now print your story on another sheet of paper. Use at least three of your New Words.

Are You Caught by Fish Facts?

Here are some books you'l swallow hook, line, and sinker:

- *The Long Lost Coelacant. and Other Living Fossils* by Aliki.
  (Thomas Y. Crowell, 197:

- *Harry and the Singing Fish* by Peter Lubach.
  (Hyperion, 1992)

Swim over to the test...

TEST-TAKING SECRETS REVEALED

Mark your answers with a sharpened, No. 2 pencil. Have several handy in case one breaks.

Look at each picture. Fill in the circle next to the word that best fits the picture.

1
- Ⓐ holes
- Ⓑ homes
- Ⓒ holds
- Ⓓ hoses

2
- Ⓐ trails
- Ⓑ fish
- Ⓒ tails
- Ⓓ heads

3
- Ⓐ swim
- Ⓑ dance
- Ⓒ dig
- Ⓓ rest

4
- Ⓐ bench
- Ⓑ playground
- Ⓒ school
- Ⓓ beach

Read each sentence. Fill in the circle next to the word that best completes the sentence.

5 A ship rides on the _____.
- Ⓐ beach
- Ⓑ see
- Ⓒ sea
- Ⓓ tails

6 The children _____ when they have been sitting too long.
- Ⓐ wiggle
- Ⓑ dance
- Ⓒ rest
- Ⓓ dig

7 As you dig the hole, it will get _____.
- Ⓐ higher
- Ⓑ deeper
- Ⓒ lower
- Ⓓ smaller

8 The hens _____ their eggs.
- Ⓐ find
- Ⓑ get
- Ⓒ put
- Ⓓ lay

9 The boys and girls began to _____ to the music.
- Ⓐ swim
- Ⓑ eat
- Ⓒ dance
- Ⓓ rest

10 There are _____ in the old shirt.
- Ⓐ fish
- Ⓑ holes
- Ⓒ colors
- Ⓓ tails

BALLET FOR FUN AND FITNESS

When you think of **ballet**, you probably think of ballerinas in **pretty** tutus. In your mind, you can see them twirling and **jumping** across a **stage**. The more they **practice**, the stronger they get.

Now picture football **players** or basketball players working out before a **game**. Football players practice running and getting out of each other's way. Basketball players practice leaping high into the air.

Some football players, basketball players, and other athletes also practice ballet to improve their game. Dancing helps them move faster and more gracefully. Ballet helps them build the **skills** that they need to be better athletes. So, if you're interested in becoming an athlete, think about taking some ballet lessons first.

CHECK THOSE DETAILS

Which is probably <u>not</u> a reason an athlete may practice ballet?

Check the best answer.

- ☐ to become more graceful
- ☐ to become stronger
- ☐ to join a dance team
- ☐ to become faster

JUMP INTO THE ALPHABET

Write the New Words in aphabetical order.

👉 Look at the first letter of each New Word. When the first letters are the same, use the second letters.

plant comes before **pr**ose

When the first two letters are the same, use the third letters.

prance comes before **pre**ach

New Words

ballet
pretty
jumping
stage
practice
players
game
skills

1. _____

2. _____

3. _____

4. _____

5. _____

6. _____

7. _____

8. _____

TODAY'S MATCH: WORDS AND MEANINGS

Use a New Word to finish each meaning. Fill in the word shapes.

1. "Leaping" means ⬜⬜⬜⬜⬜⬜⬜ .

2. People who take part in games are ⬜⬜⬜⬜⬜⬜⬜ .

3. Something that is pleasant to look at is ⬜⬜⬜⬜⬜⬜ .

4. A raised platform is a ⬜⬜⬜⬜⬜ .

5. "Abilities" means ⬜⬜⬜⬜⬜⬜ .

6. A sport or contest is a ⬜⬜⬜⬜ .

7. A kind of graceful dance is ⬜⬜⬜⬜⬜⬜ .

8. "To do something over and over" means to ⬜⬜⬜⬜⬜⬜⬜⬜ .

9

ATHLETES FILL IN THE BLANKS

Write the New Word that best completes each sentence.

1. I enjoyed watching the _____ .
   bullet   ballet   bugle

2. My sister performed on the _____ at her school.
   ballet   practice   stage

3. I need to _____ my skills.
   practice   push   put

4. He is good at _____ and running.
   practice   game   jumping

5. What a _____ picture you painted!
   game   stage   pretty

6. He showed us his basketball _____ on the court.
   skills   skits   skis

7. Which _____ do you like to play the best?
   ballet   jumping   game

8. Each of the _____ scored some points.
   players   skills   plays

FREE THE HIDDEN WORDS

Circle each New Word in the word search.

C	P	B	E	Q	Y	J	B	V
P	R	A	C	T	I	C	E	B
L	E	L	O	A	D	X	Z	T
A	T	L	I	G	A	M	E	F
Y	T	E	L	E	P	R	K	D
E	Y	T	S	K	I	L	L	S
R	F	S	T	A	G	E	S	E
S	G	N	A	M	W	A	G	U
H	J	U	M	P	I	N	G	C

New Words

ballet

pretty

jumping

stage

practice

players

game

skills

ROAD TRIPS

Both football players and ballet dancers travel to many places to perform. Imagine that you are a performer traveling to a town that you have never been to before. Write a story about your trip.

These questions will help you get started:
- What will you perform when you arrive?
- What happened while you were there?
- What did you like best about the town?

Use three of the New Words as you write your story.

DID YOU KNOW?

Ballet began in Italy about 500 years ago. Later, a French king, Louis XIV, helped to make ballet a popular form of dance. In 1661, he opened the first ballet school to train dancers.

SAY PRETTY, PLEASE!

The hand movements in dancing and other performances sometimes are a kind of sign language called *mime*. Each movement stands for a different "word." Can you guess what this mime is saying?

Answer: This mime is saying "please."

READ MORE ABOUT IT

- *Eyewitness: Sports* by Tim Hammond. (Knopf, 1988)

- *I Want to Be a Ballet Dancer* by Liza Alexander. (Western, 1993)

- *Tutu* by Audrey Chevance. (Dutton, 1991)

On your toes to the test!

TEST-DAY TIPS TOLD

Mark your answers with a sharpened, no. 2 pencil. Have several handy in case one breaks.

Look at each picture. Fill in the circle next to the word that best fits each picture.

1
- Ⓐ game
- Ⓑ football
- Ⓒ basketball
- Ⓓ ballet

3
- Ⓐ pretty
- Ⓑ ballet
- Ⓒ jumping
- Ⓓ practice

2
- Ⓐ pretty
- Ⓑ jumping
- Ⓒ ballet
- Ⓓ stage

4
- Ⓐ pretty
- Ⓑ practice
- Ⓒ game
- Ⓓ stage

Read each sentence. Fill in the circle next to the word that best completes the sentence.

5 To have special abilities is to have . . . .
- Ⓐ players
- Ⓑ practice
- Ⓒ game
- Ⓓ skills

6 Another name for a sport or contest is a . . . .
- Ⓐ ballet
- Ⓑ practice
- Ⓒ game
- Ⓓ stage

7 People who take part in games are . . . .
- Ⓐ players
- Ⓑ skills
- Ⓒ ballet
- Ⓓ practice

8 A raised platform is a . . . .
- Ⓐ practice
- Ⓑ ballet
- Ⓒ stage
- Ⓓ jumping

9 A kind of dance is . . . .
- Ⓐ jumping
- Ⓑ pretty
- Ⓒ practice
- Ⓓ ballet

10 To do something over and over is to . . . .
- Ⓐ play
- Ⓑ walk
- Ⓒ practice
- Ⓓ run

AMAZING DISCOVERY...
CHILDREN SPEAK DOZENS OF LANGUAGES

Do you **speak** English? If you do, you also know how to speak words from **dozens** of other languages! That's because English is made up of many words from **around** the world. The word *ballet* is from the French language. The Dutch gave the word *dock* to the English language. The word *zebra* is a Bantu word from Africa. *Coffee* is an Arabic word, and *kindergarten* is German.

Many English **explorers** came to the New World from the 1500s to the 1700s. At that time, there were over 2,200 languages **spoken** in North and South America. The English explorers saw many animals, foods, and **buildings** that were new to them. They had no words to **describe** these things. So they learned the words from the people who already lived here.

Do you wonder where some of your favorite words come from? Look them up in the **dictionary** to find out.

FIND THE DETAIL

Where did the word <u>zebra</u> come from?
Check the best answer.

- ❑ the Sioux language
- ❑ the Bantu language of Africa
- ❑ the French language
- ❑ the Dutch language

ALPHABET ORDERS NEW WORDS

Write the New Words in alphabetical order.

☞ Look at the beginning of each New Word. When the first letters are the same, use the second letters.

d__e__nt comes before **d__o__**

When the first two letters are the same, use the third letters.

spe__a__r comes before **spo__t__**

NEW WORDS

speak
dozens
around
explorers
spoken
buildings
describe
dictionary

1. _____   5. _____

2. _____   6. _____

3. _____   7. _____

4. _____   8. _____

MYSTERY SOLVED: WORDS MATCH MEANINGS

Use a New Word to finish each meaning. Fill in the word shapes.

1. Houses and schools are called ⬚⬚⬚⬚⬚⬚⬚⬚⬚ .

2. To say something is to ⬚⬚⬚⬚⬚ .

3. A book of words and their meanings is a ⬚⬚⬚⬚⬚⬚⬚⬚⬚⬚ .

4. A word that means "in many parts of" is ⬚⬚⬚⬚⬚⬚ .

5. People who go to new places are called ⬚⬚⬚⬚⬚⬚⬚⬚⬚ .

6. Things that are in groups of twelve are ⬚⬚⬚⬚⬚⬚ .

7. If something was said, it was ⬚⬚⬚⬚⬚⬚ .

8. To tell what something is like is to ⬚⬚⬚⬚⬚⬚⬚⬚ .

14

WORDS PLUG SENTENCE HOLES

Write the New Word that best fits in each sentence.

1. I live in one of the _____ on this street.
   dozens   buildings   explorers

2. You can see many parks _____ our town.
   around   aside   at

3. The _____ found a great treasure.
   dozens   explorers   buildings

4. Please _____ what happened.
   speak   spoken   describe

5. I looked up the word in the _____ .
   dozens   dictionary   describe

6. English was _____ by the Pilgrims.
   speak   say   spoken

7. My family eats _____ of eggs in a year.
   dozens   explorers   buildings

8. I will _____ to Grandma on the phone.
   spoken   describe   speak

SOUNDS ALONE ARE NOT THE ANSWER

☞ **Homonyms** are words that sound alike but do not have the same spelling or mean the same thing.

be and **bee**

I'd like to be a bee.

Draw lines to match the homonyms.

1. to	a. sea	5. I	e. knew
2. no	b. blew	6. whole	f. eye
3. blue	c. know	7. new	g. sew
4. see	d. two	8. so	h. hole

Use the words from above to complete these sentences.

9. Close one _____ and look at the letters with the other.

10. _____ do not know your name.

11. He was hungry, _____ he ate an apple.

12. I will _____ the rip in your dress.

15

NEWCOMERS BORROW WORDS

The English settlers in the New World also met other settlers who had come before them. They learned new words from these people, too. Here is a list of some of them:

Word	Language
cookie	Dutch
lasso	Spanish
parade	Spanish
pioneer	French
prairie	French
pretzel	German
sleigh	Dutch

READ MORE ABOUT IT

- *Who Says a Dog Goes Bow-Wow?* by Hank De Zutter. (Doubleday, 1993)
- *Why Do You Speak as You Do? A Guide to World Languages* by Kay Cooper. (Walker, 1992)

SAY IT AGAIN, SAM

People in England and the United States both speak English. But is this the same language? Not quite! Here are some American words and the English words that mean the same thing.

American English	British English
apartment	flat
elevator	lift
trunk (of a car)	boot
hood (of a car)	bonnet
subway	underground
lawyer	barrister

PUTTING WORDS IN YOUR MOUTH

 Write a report about some words that you have learned from another language. Share your report with a friend.

These questions may help you get started:

- What words from other languages have you learned lately?
- What do these words mean?
- What words would you like to know more about?

Use three New Words in your report.

Speaking of the test....

16

IMPROVE YOUR SCORE

On test day, bring your own eraser and make sure it erases cleanly.

Read each group of words. Fill in the circle next to the word or words that mean the <u>*same*</u> *as the underlined word.*

1 <u>around</u> the world
- Ⓐ on the other side
- Ⓑ in many places
- Ⓒ in a circle
- Ⓓ like a ball

2 tall <u>buildings</u>
- Ⓐ lakes
- Ⓑ people
- Ⓒ structures with walls and roofs
- Ⓓ structures with poles and flags

3 <u>spoken</u> words
- Ⓐ said
- Ⓑ heard
- Ⓒ written
- Ⓓ typed

4 <u>dozens</u> of pencils
- Ⓐ a few
- Ⓑ groups of 10
- Ⓒ a hundred
- Ⓓ groups of 12

Read each sentence. Fill in the circle next to the word that best completes the sentence.

5 I ____ two languages.
- Ⓐ speak
- Ⓑ spoken
- Ⓒ describe
- Ⓓ dictionary

6 Look up the word in your ____ .
- Ⓐ explorers
- Ⓑ buildings
- Ⓒ dictionary
- Ⓓ dozens

7 The ____ came to America many years ago.
- Ⓐ dozens
- Ⓑ explorers
- Ⓒ building
- Ⓓ dictionary

8 I cannot ____ what happened.
- Ⓐ speak
- Ⓑ spoken
- Ⓒ dictionary
- Ⓓ describe

9 He has traveled ____ the whole world.
- Ⓐ around
- Ⓑ explorers
- Ⓒ aside
- Ⓓ under

10 English is the only language ____ in our home.
- Ⓐ speak
- Ⓑ around
- Ⓒ describe
- Ⓓ spoken

WASHINGTON LEADS WINTER WARRIORS

"It was so cold the fire froze!" soldier recalls.

It was January, 1778. The War for Independence was on. George Washington led a big **army**. His men were ready to fight to be free from Great Britain. They wanted to free their **country**.

They were having a hard **winter**. The **soldiers** were very cold and tired. They were **hungry**. Many wanted to go home. George Washington was hungry, too. His soldiers saw this. They decided to stay with him.

People who lived near the army brought them food. George Washington and his men made it **through** that hard winter. He **trained** his men to be better soldiers. When it was time to fight, they would win. This land would be free.

Details, ATTENTION!

What did the men want to do?

Check the best answer.

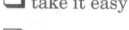

- [ ] take it easy
- [ ] eat less food
- [ ] make up their minds
- [ ] go home

ALPHABET ARMY ON THE MARCH

Print the New Words on the lines in ABC order.

☞ Look at the first letter of each New Word. When the first letters are the same, use the second letters.

three comes before **tr**uck

1. _____   5. _____

2. _____   6. _____

3. _____   7. _____

4. _____   8. _____

WORD MATCH HITS THE TARGET

Use a New Word to finish each meaning. Fill in the word shapes.

1. A man, a woman, and a girl are ⬚⬚⬚⬚⬚⬚ .

2. A group that fights in a war is an ⬚⬚⬚⬚ .

3. A cold time of year is ⬚⬚⬚⬚⬚⬚ .

4. "Showed how to or taught" means ⬚⬚⬚⬚⬚⬚⬚ .

5. A land where people live is a ⬚⬚⬚⬚⬚⬚⬚ .

6. "Needing or wanting food" means ⬚⬚⬚⬚⬚⬚ .

7. People in the army are ⬚⬚⬚⬚⬚⬚⬚ .

8. "From the beginning to the end of" means ⬚⬚⬚⬚⬚⬚⬚ .

19

MISSING WORDS SURROUNDED

Circle the word that best completes each sentence.
Then print the word on the line.

1. Last _____ my family took a trip.

       people   through   winter

2. We took a jet to another _____ .

       hungry   country   soldiers

3. Men and women in the _____ work to keep us safe.

       through   winter   army

4. George Washington's _____ helped make our land free.

       soldiers   shoulders   sold

5. Many _____ watched the parade down Main Street.

       trained   people   person

6. I was so _____ , I could have eaten a cow.

       easy   hungry   winter

7. Joey _____ his dog to do many tricks.

       tickled   trained   tried

8. The dog can jump _____ several hoops.

       threw   through   though

New Words

country

army

through

winter

trained

hungry

people

soldiers

YOU SAY YOU WANT A REVOLUTION?

Learn more about George Washington and the War for Independence. Read:

- *George Washington* by Ingri D'Aulaire. (Doubleday, 1936)

- *George Washington's Breakfast* by Jean Fritz. (Putnam, 1984)

- *George Washington and the Birth of Our Nation* by Milton Meltzer. (Watts, 1986)

SCRAMBLED WORDS HIDE SECRET MESSAGE

George Washington might have sent this secret letter to his soldiers. The New Words are mixed up to fool the enemy.

Unscramble the New Words and print them on the lines. Then read the message.

To my _____ :
elsiodsr

Thank you for staying with me _____
uhrhgot

this long _____ . You have been
twenir

_____ well. I know that you have been
nretdia

_____ . It will be worth it, because
uhngry

you will help all the _____ in our new
elppoe

_____ to be free.
ryctnou

Yours truly,

George Washington

HAVE THINGS REALLY CHANGED?
YOU BE THE JUDGE

What do you think it was like to be a child growing up when George Washington was alive? Do you think children then lived the same way you do? Write about how their lives might have been similar to or different from yours.

These questions will help you get started:
- What kinds of clothing did they wear?
- Where did they go to school?
- What kinds of houses did they live in?

Use at least three New Words in your writing.

The battle is won! March on to the test!

SCORE HIGHER ON TESTS

On test day, bring your own eraser. Make sure it erases cleanly.

Read each group of words. Fill in the circle next to the word or words that mean the <u>same</u> as the underlined word.

1 free <u>country</u>
- Ⓐ army
- Ⓑ winter
- Ⓒ nation
- Ⓓ people

2 <u>through</u> the field
- Ⓐ by
- Ⓑ at
- Ⓒ near
- Ⓓ across

3 <u>trained</u> the workers
- Ⓐ taught
- Ⓑ felt
- Ⓒ pleased
- Ⓓ liked

4 <u>soldiers</u> marched
- Ⓐ clowns
- Ⓑ guns
- Ⓒ people in the army
- Ⓓ hungry people

5 hard <u>winter</u>
- Ⓐ rock
- Ⓑ season
- Ⓒ job
- Ⓓ ice

6 thanked the <u>people</u>
- Ⓐ army
- Ⓑ country
- Ⓒ men and women
- Ⓓ animals

Read each group of words. Fill in the circle next to the word that best completes the sentence.

7 To join the army is to become one of the . . . .
- Ⓐ country
- Ⓑ club
- Ⓒ team
- Ⓓ troops

8 To be very hungry is to be . . . .
- Ⓐ playing
- Ⓑ tired
- Ⓒ fed
- Ⓓ starved

9 Winter comes just after . . . .
- Ⓐ summer
- Ⓑ fall
- Ⓒ night
- Ⓓ spring

10 Skilled athletes have been . . . .
- Ⓐ marched
- Ⓑ trained
- Ⓒ thanked
- Ⓓ after

"One slip and it's over!"

frantic shopper cries.

Do you like **fruit**? The **banana** is a fruit with a sweet **flavor**. Bananas are good for you, too.

Bananas grow on a big **plant**. The plant grows as tall as a two-story house. **Every** banana plant has one big **bunch** of bananas. Each bunch has about 150 bananas.

Banana plants grow fast. The bananas are very green when they are picked. It takes them a few months to get **ripe**. The long, long trip to the **market** gives them time to get ripe. When the bananas are ready to eat, people will buy them.

DETAILS CAN GET **UNDER** YOUR SKIN

How many bananas are in each bunch?
Check the best answer.

◯ about 15   ◯ about 150

◯ about 100   ◯ about 1,500

ALPHABET TREE
SPROUTS NEW WORDS

Print the New Words on the lines in ABC order.

☞ Look at the first letter of each New Word. When the first letters are the same, look at the second letters.

b_ag comes before **b_ug**

New Words

banana

plant

every

flavor

fruit

market

bunch

ripe

1. _____   5. _____

2. _____   6. _____

3. _____   7. _____

4. _____   8. _____

WORDS AND MEANINGS MATCH

Use a New Word to finish each meaning. Fill in the word shapes.

1. "Each one" means ⬚⬚⬚⬚⬚ .

2. "Ready to pick and use for food" means ⬚⬚⬚⬚ .

3. A place where things are sold is a ⬚⬚⬚⬚⬚⬚ .

4. A living thing such as a bush is a ⬚⬚⬚⬚⬚ .

5. Part of a plant that can taste good is the ⬚⬚⬚⬚⬚ .

6. A ripe fruit with yellow skin is a ⬚⬚⬚⬚⬚⬚ .

7. "Taste" means ⬚⬚⬚⬚⬚⬚ .

8. A group of things in one place together is a ⬚⬚⬚⬚⬚ .

No need to ripen! Fried green bananas are "fast food."

The plantain is a kind of tropical banana that is usually cooked and eaten while it is still green!

Bananas Need Your Help

Did you know that the banana plant cannot reproduce without help from people? The seeds do not grow into new plants. New plants grow from stems that are under the ground. New banana plants are hard to get started.

COMPLETED SENTENCES BEAR FRUIT

Read the sentences below. Circle the word that best completes each sentence. Then print your answers on the lines.

1. Malcolm likes to eat _____ .
   ponds   fruit   farms

2. The _____ is his favorite fruit.
   banana   bands   bunch

3. The banana has a sweet _____ .
   flag   flavor   ripe

4. A _____ of bananas grows on each plant.
   beach   bench   bunch

5. Malcolm eats at least two bananas _____ day.
   every   ever   many

6. A green banana is not _____ .
   rope   ripe   bunch

7. Bananas grow on a tall _____ .
   pants   pond   plant

8. Malcolm bought some bananas at an outdoor _____ .
   mark   market   plant

TOP BANANA SOLVES FRUIT RIDDLE

Fill in the boxes, and look in the shaded part for the answer to the riddle.

Riddle: How do you split an apple, a banana, and a peach among four children?

1. yellow fruits in a bunch
2. a store
3. a taste
4. something that grows
5. color of many apples

Answer: You make fruit _____ .

KEEP YOUR EYES
Peeled

To find out more about fruit, read these great books:

- *Bananas: From Manolo to Margie* by George Ancona. (Clarion, 1982)

- *Fruit* by Pascale De Bourgoing. (Scholastic, 1991)

- *The Seasons of Arnold's Apple Tree* by Gail Gibbons. (HarperCollins, 1984)

THE FINAL WORD ON . . . FRUIT
Writers Reveal Gut Feelings

 Everybody likes fruit.
Think about why.

These questions will help you get started:
- Which fruit do you like best?
- What does it look like?
- What does it taste like?

Now on another sheet of paper write about your favorite fruit. Use at least three of your New Words.

Join the bunch and take the test!

SECRETS TO SUCCESS ON TESTS

When looking for a word that means the same as another word, replace the given word with your choice to see if it makes sense.

Read each sentence. Fill in the circle next to the word or words that best complete the definition.

1 The <u>flavor</u> of fruit is its—
- Ⓐ color
- Ⓑ skin
- Ⓒ core
- Ⓓ taste

2 A <u>bunch</u> of something is a—
- Ⓐ market
- Ⓑ group
- Ⓒ branch
- Ⓓ plant

3 <u>Every</u> means—
- Ⓐ few
- Ⓑ none
- Ⓒ all
- Ⓓ some

4 Fruit that is <u>ripe</u> is—
- Ⓐ big
- Ⓑ ready to eat
- Ⓒ green
- Ⓓ yellow

5 A <u>market</u> is a—
- Ⓐ school
- Ⓑ gym
- Ⓒ house
- Ⓓ store

6 A <u>fruit</u> is a kind of—
- Ⓐ store
- Ⓑ room
- Ⓒ animal
- Ⓓ food

7 A <u>plant</u> is something that—
- Ⓐ grows
- Ⓑ shines
- Ⓒ eats
- Ⓓ walks

Look at each picture. Fill in the circle next to the word that best fits the picture.

8
- Ⓐ grape
- Ⓑ pear
- Ⓒ banana
- Ⓓ apple

9
- Ⓐ plant
- Ⓑ banana
- Ⓒ tree
- Ⓓ bush

10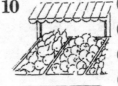
- Ⓐ plant
- Ⓑ market
- Ⓒ school
- Ⓓ home

LOOK! UP IN THE STANDS!
IT'S A BIRD! IT'S A MOOSE! IT'S A MASCOT

How would you like to watch an exciting game of **baseball** and make people laugh? It is all in a day's work for a **mascot**!

A mascot brings a **team** good luck. Some **silly** baseball mascots are the Pittsburgh Pirates' Parrot and the Seattle Mariners' Moose. The Cleveland Indians' mascot is a pink, **furry** animal with a yellow nose and yellow spots. He is called Slider because he likes to **slide** into home plate. The Philadelphia Phillies' mascot is green and furry, with a 10-inch-long **tongue**.

Mascots work hard. They get hot running around in heavy **costumes**. Just try wearing your winter coat, boots, and a paper bag over your head on a very hot day in August.

MASCOTS HAVE THE RIGHT IDEA

What is this story mainly about?

Check the best answer.

◯ how to play baseball
◯ furry animals
◯ costumes worn by mascots
◯ baseball mascots

NEW WORDS

baseball

mascot

slide

tongue

costumes

team

furry

silly

Write the New Words in alphabetical order.

☞ Look at the first letter of each New Word. When the first letters are the same, use the second letters.

sip comes before **slop**

1. _____   5. _____

2. _____   6. _____

3. _____   7. _____

4. _____   8. _____

WORDS CHEER FOR MEANINGS

Use a New Word to finish each meaning. Fill in the word shapes.

1. To move along smoothly is to ⬜⬜⬜⬜⬜.

2. A team's good-luck pet is its ⬜⬜⬜⬜⬜⬜.

3. People who work or play together as

   a group are called a ⬜⬜⬜⬜.

4. A game played with a bat and ball is ⬜⬜⬜⬜⬜⬜⬜⬜.

5. Something that is foolish is ⬜⬜⬜⬜⬜.

6. The clothes mascots wear are their ⬜⬜⬜⬜⬜⬜⬜.

7. Soft, hairy skin is ⬜⬜⬜⬜⬜.

8. The muscle in your mouth is your ⬜⬜⬜⬜⬜⬜.

29

NEW WORDS COMPLETE SENTENCES

Write the New Word that best completes each sentence.

New Words

baseball

mascot

team

silly

furry

slide

tongue

costumes

1. I had to _____ into second base.

2. We wore our _____ to the party.

3. Slider is the _____ for the Cleveland team.

4. My dad watched me play _____ .

5. Our _____ played a great game.

6. I burned my _____ on a hot drink.

7. Let me show you my _____ teddy bear.

8. Don't act _____ .

SECRET TO ANALOGIES REVEALED

An **analogy** shows how two words relate to each other.

mouse is to **animal** as **daisy** is to **plant**

The words in an analogy sometimes are opposites of each other.

hot is to **cold** as **black** is to **white**

Use a New Word to finish each of these analogies.

1. <u>bad</u> is to <u>good</u> as <u>serious</u> is to

_____

2. <u>student</u> is to <u>class</u> as <u>player</u> is to

_____

3. <u>fruit</u> is to <u>apple</u> as <u>game</u> is to

_____

4. <u>bald</u> is to <u>hairy</u> as <u>smooth</u> is to

_____

PLAY BALL!

Write a note inviting a friend to go with you to a baseball game.

These questions may help you get your note started:

- Where will you go to see the game?
- Which teams will be playing?
- What should you take with you?

Use three of the New Words in your note.

WHO'S ON FIRST?

In 1974, the San Diego Padres' Chicken was the first silly mascot to really have fun with the fans.

DON'T STRIKE OUT!

READ:

- *At the Crack of the Bat* by Lillian Morrison. (Hyperion, 1992)
- *Baseball Days* by Henry Horenstein. (Little, Brown, 1994)
- *Baseball Is Our Game* by Joan Downing. (Children's Press, 1982)
- "Mascot Madness." (*Sports Illustrated for Kids*, May, 1992)

A WEIGHTY QUESTION

How much do you think a mascot's costume weighs?

Answer: About 40 pounds!

Score big on the test!

TEST-TAKING SECRETS REVEALED

Be sure to fill in the whole answer circle, but do not spend too much time on each one.

Read each group of words. Fill in the circle next to the word or words that mean the *same* as the underlined word.

1 play for a <u>team</u>
- Ⓐ band
- Ⓑ people who play together
- Ⓒ parade
- Ⓓ family of animals

2 a <u>silly</u> clown
- Ⓐ funny
- Ⓑ painted
- Ⓒ sad
- Ⓓ tall

3 <u>furry</u> animal
- Ⓐ large
- Ⓑ small
- Ⓒ covered with feathers
- Ⓓ covered with soft hair

4 Halloween <u>costumes</u>
- Ⓐ kind of food
- Ⓑ kind of clothes
- Ⓒ lanterns
- Ⓓ bags

Read each sentence. Fill in the circle next to the word that best completes the sentence.

5 To slip along quickly with your feet is to . . . .
- Ⓐ team
- Ⓑ slide
- Ⓒ trip
- Ⓓ walk

6 The person who is to bring good luck to a team is called a . . . .
- Ⓐ baseball
- Ⓑ furry
- Ⓒ team
- Ⓓ mascot

7 A game played with a bat and ball is called . . . .
- Ⓐ basketball
- Ⓑ football
- Ⓒ baseball
- Ⓓ volleyball

8 The muscle in your mouth is called a . . . .
- Ⓐ teeth
- Ⓑ tongue
- Ⓒ tune
- Ⓓ tutu

9 A group of players all on the same side is called a . . . .
- Ⓐ baseball
- Ⓑ tongue
- Ⓒ mascot
- Ⓓ team

10 When you can't stop laughing, you are being . . . .
- Ⓐ silly
- Ⓑ angry
- Ⓒ costumes
- Ⓓ furry

Mother Goose Found!
Wild Chase Ends

What rhymes have you heard? Have you heard "Jack and Jill" or "Humpty Dumpty"? **Almost** all of us have heard **rhymes** like these. They are called **nursery** rhymes or Mother Goose rhymes.

Who is Mother Goose? Who wrote these **poems**? What is the answer to this mystery?

Mother Goose rhymes were first **printed** in the 1700's, around the time of George Washington. These rhymes were for children. They were put in **small** books. As time went on, more and more little poems were **added**. But the real Mother Goose was a mystery.

Now there are many Mother Goose Rhymes. They come from many times and many **places**. The truth about Mother Goose will never be known. Think of Mother Goose as more than one person. She is many people from different times and places. She is everyone who ever wrote a nursery rhyme.

"My goose is cooked!"
exclaims bird.

Story Holds Key to Main Idea

What is this story mainly about?

Check the best answer.

○ a very old goose
○ George Washington's mother
○ how some rhymes came to be
○ the story of "Jack and Jill"

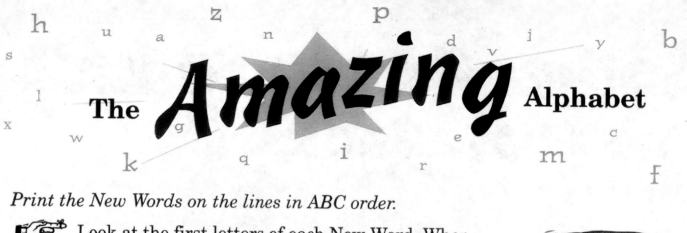

The Amazing Alphabet

Print the New Words on the lines in ABC order.

☞ Look at the first letters of each New Word. When the first letters are the same, use the second letters.

pl_ay comes before **p_ole**

1. _____   5. _____

2. _____   6. _____

3. _____   7. _____

4. _____   8. _____

New Words

almost
nursery
printed
small   places
rhymes
added
poems

Hidden Meanings Can Be Found

Use a New Word to finish each meaning. Fill in the word shapes.

1. "Nearly" means ☐☐☐☐☐☐ .

2. "Spaces where things are" means ☐☐☐☐☐☐ .

3. A room for little children is a ☐☐☐☐☐☐☐ .

4. Poems that use words with the same end sounds are ☐☐☐☐☐☐ .

5. "Made into a book" means ☐☐☐☐☐☐☐ .

6. "Little" means ☐☐☐☐☐ .

7. Nursery rhymes are ☐☐☐☐☐☐ .

8. "Were put with others" means ☐☐☐☐☐ .

Cure Found

For Incomplete Sentences!

Mysterious illness disappears after girl does homework.

Finish these sentences. Print a New Word on each line.

1. Jack and Jill is a _____ rhyme.

2. Nursery rhymes are short _____ .

3. The word <u>pet</u> _____ with <u>set</u>.

4. Newspapers and books are things that

   are _____ .

5. Mary is _____ eight years old.

6. A mouse is a _____ animal.

7. It is hard to reach things in high _____ .

8. Mom _____ two eggs to the mix.

PUZZLER

Use your New Words to complete the crossword puzzle.

New Words

nursery   added   almost   places

rhymes   printed   small   poems

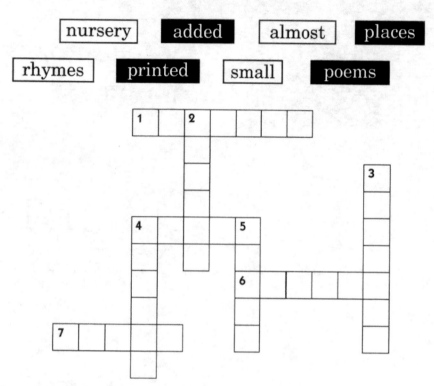

Across

1. a room for little children
4. what nursery rhymes are
6. nearly
7. were put with others

Down

2. *cat* ____ with *bat*
3. made into a book
4. spaces where things are
5. not big; little

DON'T BE A BIRD BRAIN

Read: • *The Real Mother Goose.*

(Checkerboard Press, 1944)

Watch: • *The Truth About Mother Goose.*

(Walt Disney movie)

HELP WANTED

Write Your Own Nursery Rhyme and Become the New Mother Goose

These questions will help you get started on the path to fame and fortune as the new Mother Goose:

• Who or what is your poem about?
• What happens?
• Is it strange or funny?

Now, print your nursery rhyme on another sheet of paper. Use three of your New Words. If you want, draw a picture to go along with your poem.

You're ready for the test!

TEST-DAY TIPS TOLD

When looking for a word that means the same as another word, don't be fooled by a choice that means the opposite.

Read each group of words. Fill in the circle next to the word that means the <u>same</u> as the underlined word.

1 <u>almost</u> here
- Ⓐ nearly
- Ⓑ also
- Ⓒ never
- Ⓓ always

2 a <u>small</u> bug
- Ⓐ happy
- Ⓑ huge
- Ⓒ little
- Ⓓ many

3 the little <u>poems</u>
- Ⓐ places
- Ⓑ books
- Ⓒ persons
- Ⓓ rhymes

4 <u>nursery</u> rhymes
- Ⓐ children's room
- Ⓑ school
- Ⓒ poem
- Ⓓ person

5 more were <u>added</u>
- Ⓐ smelled
- Ⓑ printed
- Ⓒ heard
- Ⓓ put in

6 books were <u>printed</u>
- Ⓐ added
- Ⓑ made
- Ⓒ heard
- Ⓓ grown

Read each sentence below. Fill in the circle next to the word that best completes the sentence.

7 When you read nursery rhymes, you are reading _____.
- Ⓐ pens
- Ⓑ places
- Ⓒ poems
- Ⓓ persons

8 Mother Goose rhymes come from many _____.
- Ⓐ schools
- Ⓑ rooms
- Ⓒ places
- Ⓓ poems

9 Many little poems have been _____ to the Mother Goose rhymes.
- Ⓐ added
- Ⓑ pasted
- Ⓒ glued
- Ⓓ joined

10 Books can be _____ in many sizes.
- Ⓐ grown
- Ⓑ printed
- Ⓒ heard
- Ⓓ added

SNAKE'S EGGS READY TO CRACK.

" I THOUGHT

I'D NEVER

GET OUT!"

*complains
baby snake.*

Did you know that snakes come from eggs? There are two ways that snakes come out of their eggs.

In one way, the eggs stay inside the mother. At first, these eggs look like **bubbles**. The mother lays them as soon as they are ready to hatch. The baby snakes move around outside right away.

Other snakes lay their eggs and then let them sit for a while. The **shells** are soft at first. Then they get harder. When the baby snake is ready, it rips **open** the shell with a tooth. This tooth **sticks** out in **front** of the baby's **mouth**.

Mother snakes do not need to take care of their babies. Baby snakes can do **everything** for **themselves**. They are on their own when they leave their eggs.

Story Hatches Main Idea

What would be a good new title for this story?

Check the best answer.

○ "How Snakes Make Bubbles"

○ "Baby Snakes Have Big Teeth"

○ "A Funny Egg"

○ "The Eggs of Snakes"

ALPHABET CAN'T BE BEAT

New Words

bubbles

shells

open

sticks

themselves

mouth

front

everything

Print the New Words on the lines in ABC order.

☞ Look at the first letter of each New Word. When the first letters are the same, look at the second letters.

s̲hape comes before st̲op

1. _____   5. _____

2. _____   6. _____

3. _____   7. _____

4. _____   8. _____

WHICH CAME FIRST, THE *MEANING* OR THE *WORD*?

Use a New Word to finish each meaning. Fill in the word shapes.

1. "All things" means ⬜⬜⬜⬜⬜⬜⬜⬜⬜⬜ .

2. Balls of air are ⬜⬜⬜⬜⬜⬜⬜ .

3. The soft or hard coverings of eggs are ⬜⬜⬜⬜⬜⬜ .

4. "Not shut" means ⬜⬜⬜⬜ .

5. The part of your body through which you take in food is called your ⬜⬜⬜⬜⬜ .

6. The part that is not in the back is the ⬜⬜⬜⬜⬜ .

7. "Their own or true selves" means ⬜⬜⬜⬜⬜⬜⬜⬜⬜⬜ .

8. "Reaches or extends out" means ⬜⬜⬜⬜⬜⬜ .

39

FROGS LEAP
AT CHANCE TO COMPLETE SENTENCES

Finish the sentences below. Print the New Words on the lines.

New Words			
mouth	everything	front	open
sticks	themselves	bubbles	shells

1. The coverings, or _____, of frogs' eggs are soft.

2. Baby frogs come out of eggs all by _____ .

3. The baby is round in the _____ and has a tail in the back.

4. A frog's big _____ is ready for a bite to eat.

5. When a fly comes by, the frog's mouth pops _____ .

6. The frog _____ its tongue out of its mouth and flips the fly in.

7. At last, the frog has eaten _____ it wants.

8. Then the frog jumps back into the water, making _____ as it goes.

SNAKE NONSENSE

Here are some common myths about snakes:

- Snakes suck the milk from cows.
- Snakes roll around like hoops chasing after people.
- Snakes swallow their babies to keep them safe.
- If you hit a snake, it will shatter like glass and then put itself back together.

BE THE ENVY OF YOUR FRIENDS!

Learn more about snakes by reading these books:

- *Snake* by Caroline Arnold. (William Morrow, 1991)
- *The Moon and I* by Betsy Byars. (Simon and Schuster, 1992)

ANTONYM PUZZLE FINALLY SOLVED

👉 **Antonyms** are words that mean the opposite of each other.

enter and **exit**

Fill in the boxes with antonyms from the Word List.
The first one is done for you.

Word List
nothing
others
closed
rear
off

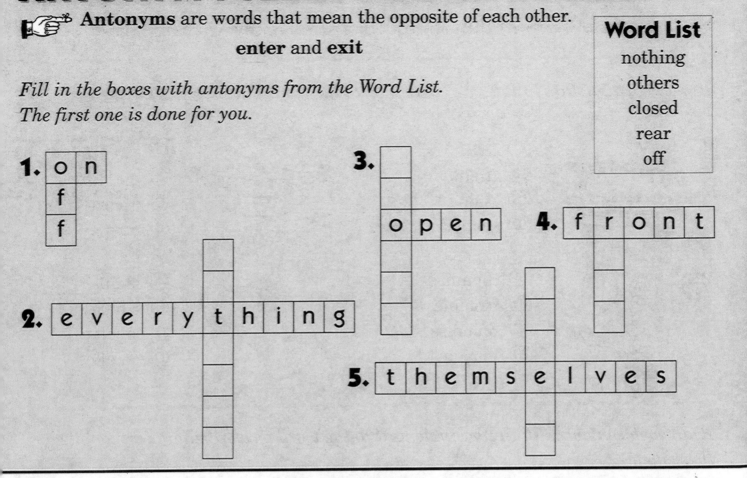

1. o n
   f
   f

2. e v e r y t h i n g

3. o p e n

4. f r o n t

5. t h e m s e l v e s

NEW ANIMALS CREATED IN WORD EXPERIMENT!

ANIMAL + ANIMAL = "ADDIMAL"

📓 Pick two or more animals. Put them together and make a funny, new animal. You may choose from these or other animals:

horse	tiger	snake	lion
goat	dog	bear	cat
elephant	bee	deer	

elephant + bee = elebee

Tell all about your "addimal" on another sheet of paper. Then draw a picture of your "addimal." Use at least three New Words.

Slither over to the test!

SECRETS TO SUCCESS ON TESTS

Be careful of answers that look or sound alike. Say the words to yourself.

Look at each picture. Fill in the circle next to the word that best fits the picture.

1
- Ⓐ back
- Ⓑ front
- Ⓒ side
- Ⓓ under

3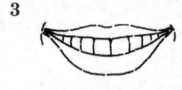
- Ⓐ month
- Ⓑ mouth
- Ⓒ mouse
- Ⓓ money

2
- Ⓐ bunnies
- Ⓑ troubles
- Ⓒ bubbles
- Ⓓ buggies

4
- Ⓐ smiles
- Ⓑ shakes
- Ⓒ shells
- Ⓓ snakes

Read each sentence. Fill in the circle next to the word or words that best complete the sentence.

5 The main door of a house is usually the one that faces the . . . .
- Ⓐ back
- Ⓑ front
- Ⓒ basement
- Ⓓ upstairs

6 The hard coverings of eggs are called . . . .
- Ⓐ shells
- Ⓑ sacks
- Ⓒ bubbles
- Ⓓ bags

7 A door that is not closed is . . . .
- Ⓐ far
- Ⓑ near
- Ⓒ shut
- Ⓓ open

8 A word that is used to talk about a group of people is . . . .
- Ⓐ everything
- Ⓑ themselves
- Ⓒ almost
- Ⓓ through

9 Something that comes through . . . .
- Ⓐ stays with
- Ⓑ pushes away
- Ⓒ sticks out
- Ⓓ puts in

10 When you have all that you need, you have . . . .
- Ⓐ shells
- Ⓑ themselves
- Ⓒ bubbles
- Ⓓ everything

ANCIENT AZTEC KINGDOM ONCE RULED MEXICO

ISLAND CITY KEPT AZTECS SAFE

L ong ago in Mexico there lived a **strong** people. They were the Aztecs. Their **kingdom** was **beautiful**. They had a city in the **center** of a lake. Other people could not get into their city. For a long time, the Aztecs were safe.

The Aztecs sent soldiers all over the land. They took what they wanted. They became rich.

Later, soldiers came from far away. They **fought** the Aztecs. They **tore** down their city. But Aztecs still live today. The Aztecs are still a part of the people of Mexico.

Some good things we have now came from the Aztecs. Do you drink **cocoa**? If you do, you can thank the Aztecs. They made the hot drink first.

Today the Mexican people still celebrate Aztec culture.

EXCITING MAIN IDEA FOUND IN AZTEC STORY!

What is this story mainly about?
Check the best answer.

☐ a strong group of people
☐ how soldiers become rich
☐ how cocoa is made
☐ a city in the center of the lake

NEW WORDS SHOW ALPHABETICAL ORDER

Print the New Words on the lines in ABC order.

☞ Look at the first letter of each New Word. When the first letters are the same, look at the second letters.

car comes before **c<u>o</u>at**

1. _____   5. _____

2. _____   6. _____

3. _____   7. _____

4. _____   8. _____

New Words

fought
beautiful
center
kingdom
strong
cocoa
later
tore

NEW WORDS MATCH OLD MEANINGS

Use a New Word to finish each meaning.
Fill in the word shapes.

1. A sweet, brown, hot drink is ☐☐☐☐☐ .

2. "Pretty" means ☐☐☐☐☐☐☐☐☐ .

3. "Full of power, or mighty" means ☐☐☐☐☐☐ .

4. "After a time" means ☐☐☐☐☐ .

5. "Middle" means ☐☐☐☐☐☐ .

6. "Had a fight" means ☐☐☐☐☐☐ .

7. A land ruled by a king is a ☐☐☐☐☐☐☐ .

8. "Ripped or took apart" means ☐☐☐☐ .

Ancient Empires

The most famous civilizations in the ancient Americas were the Aztec, the Inca, and the Maya.

WORDS NEEDED TO FILL SENTENCE HOLES

Finish the sentences below. Print a New Word on each line.

1. Do you want a cup of hot _____ ?

2. We will wash the dishes now and go to the store _____ .

3. Oh! That sunset is _____ .

4. It would take a _____ person to pick up that rock.

5. Go to the _____ of the circle.

6. There is a big hole where Joe _____ his shirt.

7. The king rode through the land to meet the people of his _____ .

8. Many people have _____ in wars.

Ancient Mysteries

• The pyramids built by the ancient Aztecs were almost identical to the ones built in ancient Egypt. However, scientists do not believe there is any connection between the two cultures.

• The Aztecs played a game called Pok-a-tok. It was similar to modern basketball, but you could only touch the ball with your hip!

WORDS OF A FEATHER GROUP TOGETHER

Each New Word below helps describe a group.
Circle the three words that belong in each group.

1. part of a <u>kingdom</u>

land   people   strong   king

2. things that can be done <u>later</u>

talking   string   running   playing

3. could be in the <u>center</u> of a room

moon   chair   rug   table

Reporter Discovers New Kingdom

 Imagine that you are an explorer and discover a lost civilization. Write a report about this kingdom. Pretend your report will appear in the school newspaper.

These questions will help you get started:
- What does the kingdom look like?
- Who lives there?
- What do the people do all day?

Now write your report on another sheet of paper. Use at least three New Words in the report.

Be the First on Your Block

Learn more about the Aztecs. Read these interesting books:

- *The Hungry Woman: Myth and Legends of the Aztecs* by John Bierhorst. (William Morrow, 1993)

- *The Feathered Serpent* by Scott O'Dell. (Houghton Mifflin, 1981)

- *The Aztecs* by Donna A. Shepherd. (Watts, 1992)

IMPROVE YOUR SCORE

When looking for a word that means the opposite of another word, don't be fooled by a choice that means the same.

Read each group of words. Fill in the circle next to the word that means the <u>opposite</u> of the underlined word.

1 <u>strong</u> wind
- Ⓐ powerful
- Ⓑ loud
- Ⓒ cold
- Ⓓ weak

2 <u>center</u> of the room
- Ⓐ under
- Ⓑ middle
- Ⓒ edge
- Ⓓ over

3 <u>tore</u> the book
- Ⓐ repaired
- Ⓑ make
- Ⓒ painted
- Ⓓ fought

4 left <u>later</u>
- Ⓐ almost
- Ⓑ after
- Ⓒ sooner
- Ⓓ during

5 <u>beautiful</u> sunset
- Ⓐ pretty
- Ⓑ ugly
- Ⓒ nice
- Ⓓ red

Read each sentence. Fill in the circle next to the word that best completes the sentence.

6 A king rules his _____.
- Ⓐ center
- Ⓑ market
- Ⓒ city
- Ⓓ kingdom

7 Things that must be done by now cannot be done _____.
- Ⓐ during
- Ⓑ later
- Ⓒ before
- Ⓓ ladder

8 We drank cups of hot _____.
- Ⓐ cold
- Ⓑ strong
- Ⓒ cocoa
- Ⓓ bread

9 The soldiers _____ for their country.
- Ⓐ strong
- Ⓑ fought
- Ⓒ tore
- Ⓓ forgot

10 The Aztecs built a _____ city in the middle of a lake.
- Ⓐ later
- Ⓑ cold
- Ⓒ center
- Ⓓ beautiful

47

NERD ALERT!

TV'S SUPER NERD REALLY MATTERS

Get ready for Super Nerd! Each week, Jaleel White **appears** as Steve Urkel on the hit TV show "Family Matters." Urkel has crashed through the ceiling, fallen off the roof, and smashed through a coffee table. He has thrown a ball, *and himself*, through his neighbor's window. And that's just a quick look at Urkel's **antics**.

Where Urkel **lurks**, trouble is probably **nearby**. Maybe that's because Urkel is a **genius** who has his head in the clouds. Jaleel White, the **actor** who plays Urkel, has his head in show business. His heart is in acting, too. He is nothing like a nerd in real life.

Jaleel started acting when he was only three. He has done ads, TV shows, and **movies**. Maybe you've seen him as a **guest** on other TV shows.

Next time you hear "Nerd alert," watch out. Steve Urkel is probably just around the corner.

"DID I DO THAT?"
Urkel whines.

MAIN IDEA FOUND IN STORY

What is this story mainly about?

Check the best answer.

- ☐ Jaleel White
- ☐ "Family Matters"
- ☐ Steve Urkel
- ☐ Super Nerds

THINK ALPHABETICALLY

Write the New Words in alphabetical order.

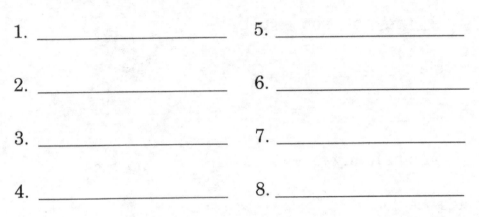 Look at the first letter of each New Word. When the first letters are the same, use the second letters.

a<u>n</u>t comes before **a<u>p</u>ron**

1. _____

2. _____

3. _____

4. _____

5. _____

6. _____

7. _____

8. _____

appears
antics
lurks
nearby
genius
actor
movies
guest

★ ★

HELP FIND WORD MEANINGS

Use a New Word to finish each meaning. Fill in the word shapes.

1. Playful or silly actions are ☐☐☐☐☐ .

2. Another word for *near* is ☐☐☐☐☐☐ .

3. "Comes into sight" means ☐☐☐☐☐☐☐ .

4. Shows put on film are called ☐☐☐☐☐☐ .

5. If something "lies in wait," it ☐☐☐☐☐ .

6. A person who plays a part in a movie is an ☐☐☐☐☐ .

7. A person who comes to visit is a ☐☐☐☐☐ .

8. A very smart person may be a ☐☐☐☐☐☐ .

WORDS FILL SENTENCE HOLES

Write the New Word that best completes each sentence.

1. Jaleel White is an _____ in "Family Matters."

2. I laugh every week at his_____ .

3. Jaleel has also played in _____ .

4. He has been a _____ on other shows, too.

5. Where Steve Urkel is, trouble is _____.

6. You may not know that he is a _____ .

7. The actor _____ only in funny movies.

8. He _____ outside the door.

New Words

appears

antics

lurks

nearby

genius

actor

movies

guest

FREE THE HIDDEN WORDS

Circle each New Word in the word search.

A	Y	B	A	N	T	I	C	S
O	A	X	C	D	J	M	Z	P
J	P	N	T	B	H	P	L	G
W	P	M	O	V	I	E	S	U
N	E	A	R	B	Y	A	G	E
Q	A	C	V	C	E	R	K	S
D	R	E	L	U	R	K	S	T
H	S	G	E	N	I	U	S	F
G	I	T	K	P	S	U	M	O

"CAN I DO THAT?" ASKS WRITER

Some of us may find it hard to act on a stage. Jaleel White finds it easy. But there are other things that are hard for him to do. What do you find hard to do? Write about it.

These questions will help you get started:
- Why is it hard for you to do this thing?
- How does trying to do it make you feel?
- How can you make it easier to do?

Use three of the New Words in your writing.

★ ★ ★ ★ ★ ★ ★ ★ ★ ★ ★ ★ ★ ★ ★ ★

NOT FOR NERDS ONLY

★ Jaleel once had his own television show, "The Jaleel White Special."

★ Jaleel did a TV special called "President Clinton: Answering Children's Questions Live from the White House."

DON'T BE A NERD!

READ:

- *How It Works: Television and Video* by Ian Graham. (Gloucester Press, 1991)

- *Steve Urkel's Super Cool Guide to Success* by C. M. Appleton. (Scholastic, 1992)

- *TV and Video Technology* by Mark Lambert. (Watts, 1990)

- *Writing Your Own Plays: Creating, Adapting, Improvising* by Carol Korty. (Scribners, 1986)

Turn off the tube and take the test!

SCORE HIGHER ON TESTS

Look over your test a last time to make sure you did not miss any questions and that your answers can be easily read by the teacher.

Read each sentence below. Fill in the circle next to the word or words that mean the <u>*same*</u> *as the underlined word.*

1 To be <u>nearby</u> is to be—
Ⓐ sad
Ⓑ far
Ⓒ good
Ⓓ close

2 To be a <u>guest</u> is to be a—
Ⓐ teacher
Ⓑ visitor
Ⓒ parent
Ⓓ genius

3 A clown's <u>antics</u> are his—
Ⓐ pranks
Ⓑ aunts
Ⓒ insects
Ⓓ animals

4 To go to the <u>movies</u> is to see—
Ⓐ a game
Ⓑ a picnic
Ⓒ pictures
Ⓓ races

Read each sentence. Fill in the circle next to the word that best completes the sentence.

5 Jaleel has been an ____ since he was three years old.
Ⓐ action
Ⓑ actor
Ⓒ act
Ⓓ active

6 He ____ in a TV show every week.
Ⓐ lurks
Ⓑ movies
Ⓒ appears
Ⓓ nearby

7 A robber ____ outside the store.
Ⓐ lurks
Ⓑ movies
Ⓒ nearby
Ⓓ antics

8 My father is a ____ at fixing cars.
Ⓐ teacher
Ⓑ visitor
Ⓒ guest
Ⓓ genius

9 I will be ____ if you need me.
Ⓐ neat
Ⓑ never
Ⓒ nearly
Ⓓ nearby

10 Stop your ____ and get to work!
Ⓐ lurks
Ⓑ genius
Ⓒ antics
Ⓓ appears

STOP

Flower Power
AMAZING FLOWER HAS A POWERFUL SMELL

This flower grows as tall as a teenager!

Try to imagine a huge **flower**. The biggest flower in the **world** is the rafflesia (ra FLEE zhuh). It is very **heavy**. It weighs about four pounds! If you picked it up, it would feel like a small watermelon. If you pinned this flower on yourself, only a small part of you would show.

This flower is strange in other ways, too. It is **ugly**, not pretty like other flowers. It does not **smell** good. It can be **sticky**. Only flies like this flower. They lay their eggs on it. It **robs** other plants for its food. Be **thankful**! This flower grows far away in Indonesia.

ORDER FOUND IN FLOWER STORY

What does the story tell about first?

Check the best answer.

◯ how flies like the flower   ◯ the size of the flower

◯ the place the flower grows   ◯ the smell of the flower

ALPHABET MAKES WORDS GROW!

New Words

flower

ugly

smell

world

robs

sticky

heavy

thankful

Print the New Words on the lines in ABC order.

☞ Look at the first letter of each New Word. When the first letters are the same, look at the second letters.

small comes before **st**ack

1. _____   5. _____

2. _____   6. _____

3. _____   7. _____

4. _____   8. _____

CONNECTION FOUND BETWEEN WORDS AND MEANINGS!

Use a New Word to finish each meaning.
Fill in the word shapes.

1. Another word for our earth is ⬜⬜⬜⬜⬜ .

2. Something hard to lift is ⬜⬜⬜⬜⬜ .

3. To "have an odor" means to ⬜⬜⬜⬜⬜ .

4. "Holding to other things like glue" means ⬜⬜⬜⬜⬜⬜ .

5. "Feeling thanks" means ⬜⬜⬜⬜⬜⬜⬜⬜ .

6. The part of the plant that grows from the bud is the ⬜⬜⬜⬜⬜⬜ .

7. A thing that is not at all pretty is ⬜⬜⬜⬜ .

8. "Takes from others" means ⬜⬜⬜⬜ .

MISSING WORDS CAUSE SENTENCE HOLES

Finish the sentences. Print a New Word on each line.

1. What one person thinks is pretty, another might think is _____ .

2. The biggest flower in the world does not _____ too good.

3. Cindy's suitcase was too _____ to carry.

4. The jet is going around the _____ .

5. You should be _____ for all you have.

6. Pick a pretty _____ for me.

7. That glue is very _____ .

8. Someone who _____ a bank is breaking the law.

The Flower Power Story Hour

Read 'em and grow:

- *The Legend of the Indian Paintbrush* by Tomie De Paola. (Putnam, 1991)

- *What's Your Favorite Flower?* by Allan Fowler. (Children's Press, 1992)

- *The Rose in My Garden* by Arnold Lobel. (Greenwillow, 1984)

THE UNTOLD STORY OF PLANTS

- Some plants, like the Venus' flytrap or the sundew, catch and eat insects!

- Most plants need insects such as bees or butterflies to spread their pollen. Plants grow flowers to attract these insect helpers.

☞ **Antonyms** are words that mean the opposite of each other.

over and **under**

Draw lines to match the antonyms below.

1. heavy   a. cold
2. up   b. winter
3. hot   c. down
4. summer   d. in
5. out   e. light

6. open   a. come
7. ugly   b. back
8. leave   c. closed
9. same   d. opposite
10. front   e. pretty

Skunk Trial Begins

Look at the picture to the right.
Read the facts below about skunks.
Do you think the skunk is a good animal
or a bad animal?

- lives under the ground
- about the size of a cat
- has thick fur
- may take over a woodchuck's home
- fur used to make coats
- gives off strong smell when afraid
- eats fruit, berries, bugs, mice, and rats

On another sheet of paper, write four sentences that show someone else that the skunk is good or that the skunk is bad. Use at least three New Words.

You came out smelling like a rose! You may now take the test.

TEST-TAKING SECRETS REVEALED

Relax! Take a few deep breaths before you begin. This will help you do better on the test.

Look at each picture. Fill in the circle next to the word that best fits the picture.

1
- Ⓐ heavy
- Ⓑ ugly
- Ⓒ thankful
- Ⓓ sticky

3
- Ⓐ worth
- Ⓑ world
- Ⓒ wood
- Ⓓ would

2
- Ⓐ flatter
- Ⓑ fewer
- Ⓒ flower
- Ⓓ fatter

4
- Ⓐ smell
- Ⓑ small
- Ⓒ sticky
- Ⓓ robs

Read each group of words. Fill in the circle next to the word or words that mean the <u>same</u> as the underlined word.

5 <u>heavy</u> box
- Ⓐ sticky
- Ⓑ hard to close
- Ⓒ cold
- Ⓓ hard to lift

7 an <u>ugly</u> thing
- Ⓐ sick
- Ⓑ sticky
- Ⓒ bad looking
- Ⓓ beautiful

9 <u>sticky</u> paper
- Ⓐ gummy
- Ⓑ beautiful
- Ⓒ ugly
- Ⓓ heavy

6 <u>thankful</u> for your help
- Ⓐ sad
- Ⓑ glad
- Ⓒ sorry
- Ⓓ sleepy

8 <u>robs</u> the store
- Ⓐ shines
- Ⓑ smells
- Ⓒ takes from
- Ⓓ gives to

10 smell the <u>flower</u>
- Ⓐ world
- Ⓑ blossom
- Ⓒ watermelon
- Ⓓ egg

"I HAVE A DREAM!"
THE DREAM OF DR. MARTIN LUTHER KING, JR.

Dr. Martin Luther King, Jr., had a **dream**. It was a dream for our country. He wanted **laws** to be **fair**. He thought all people should have the same **freedom**. It should not **matter** what color their skin was. But a law said that African Americans had to sit in the back of a bus. They could not eat where white people ate. African American children could not go to school with white children. Laws made it harder for **poor** people to **vote**, too.

Dr. King knew these laws were **wrong**. He worked hard to change them. He did not use violence. In time, many laws were changed. Martin Luther King, Jr., was a man who worked to make his dreams come true.

Life Story Has Meaning

Which of these best states the main idea?
Check the best answer.

☐ People with little money found it hard to vote.

☐ African Americans and whites could not eat at the same places.

☐ Dr. Martin Luther King, Jr., helped get laws changed.

☐ Dr. Martin Luther King, Jr., did not use violence.

ALPHABETICAL ORDER

Print the New Words on the lines in ABC order.

☞ Look at the first letter of each New Word. When the first letters are the same, look at the second letters.

fa̲r comes before **fr̲iend**

1. _____   5. _____

2. _____   6. _____

3. _____   7. _____

4. _____   8. _____

New Words

dream

matter

laws

wrong

fair

freedom

vote

poor

CONNECTION FOUND
BETWEEN WORDS AND MEANINGS

Use a New Word to finish each meaning. Fill in the word shapes.

1. Rules that tell what people can do are ☐☐☐☐ .

2. To choose or to say whom you want to win is to ☐☐☐☐ .

3. The opposite of "right" is ☐☐☐☐☐ .

4. To have very little is to be ☐☐☐☐ .

5. To "make a difference" means to ☐☐☐☐☐☐ .

6. If you can choose what you want to do, you have ☐☐☐☐☐☐☐ .

7. If something is the same for everyone, it is ☐☐☐☐ .

8. An idea or hope for a better life is a ☐☐☐☐☐ .

WORD EXPERT FILLS SENTENCE HOLES!

Finish the sentences below. Print a New Word on each line.

1. People who have very little money are _____ .

2. The teacher was strict but also _____ .

3. Dr. Martin Luther King, Jr., fought for _____ .

4. People go to jail when they break _____ .

5. In November, people _____ on Election Day.

6. Dr. King taught that skin color should not _____ .

7. It is _____ to hurt someone.

8. What is your _____ for the future?

New Words

poor

freedom

matter

vote

fair

dream

wrong

laws

THE LIFE OF A HERO

- Dr. Martin Luther King, Jr., started college at the age of fifteen.

- Dr. Martin Luther King, Jr., was arrested and put in jail many times while fighting for his beliefs.

Learn More About Dr. Martin Luther King, Jr.

Read these books:

- *Martin Luther King, Jr.* by Jean Darby. (Lerner, 1990)

- *Martin Luther King, Jr., and the March Toward Freedom* by Rita Hakim. (Millbrook, 1991)

- *The Life and Words of Martin Luther King, Jr.* by Ira Peck. (Scholastic, 1991)

PUZZLING ? EVIDENCE

Use the New Words to finish the puzzle.

ACROSS

3. not right

4. to choose

5. right to do as a person wishes

7. make a difference

DOWN

1. an idea about things to come

2. not rich

5. right and just

6. rules

Need help? Use the glossary on page 103.

BE A LEGEND IN YOUR OWN MIND!

What if you were elected to be the head of our country? Think about what you would do if you became the leader of the land. These questions will help:

- Why would people vote for you?
- What would be your first act?
- What is the most important problem you would work on?

Now write a report for the newspaper that tells how you became the head of the country, and what you plan to do. Use at least three New Words.

You are free to take the test!

TEST-DAY TIPS TOLD

Look over the entire test before you begin. Check to see what you will be doing.

Read each group of words. Fill in the circle next to the word that mean the <u>opposite</u> of the underlined word.

1 <u>poor</u> people
- Ⓐ strong
- Ⓑ rich
- Ⓒ needy
- Ⓓ fair

2 <u>wrong</u> answer
- Ⓐ poor
- Ⓑ fair
- Ⓒ incorrect
- Ⓓ right

3 <u>fair</u> laws
- Ⓐ good
- Ⓑ vote
- Ⓒ bad
- Ⓓ strong

Read each sentence. Fill in the circle next to the word that best completes the sentence.

4 When a person thinks of how things could be, he or she has a . . . .
- Ⓐ drum
- Ⓑ dream
- Ⓒ laws
- Ⓓ vote

5 When we break the country's rules, we are not obeying the . . . .
- Ⓐ dream
- Ⓑ school
- Ⓒ people
- Ⓓ laws

6 To enjoy your rights is to have . . . .
- Ⓐ laws
- Ⓑ freedom
- Ⓒ money
- Ⓓ country

7 When things make a difference, they . . . .
- Ⓐ matter
- Ⓑ wrong
- Ⓒ vote
- Ⓓ dream

8 To help choose a leader is to . . . .
- Ⓐ dream
- Ⓑ lead
- Ⓒ rob
- Ⓓ vote

9 If you treat others in the right way, you will be . . . .
- Ⓐ wrong
- Ⓑ poor
- Ⓒ fair
- Ⓓ bad

10 If the answer is not right, it must be . . . .
- Ⓐ wrong
- Ⓑ right
- Ⓒ poor
- Ⓓ strong

62

HAVE YOU EVER SEEN A DRAGON FLY?
Amazing Creatures Really Exist!

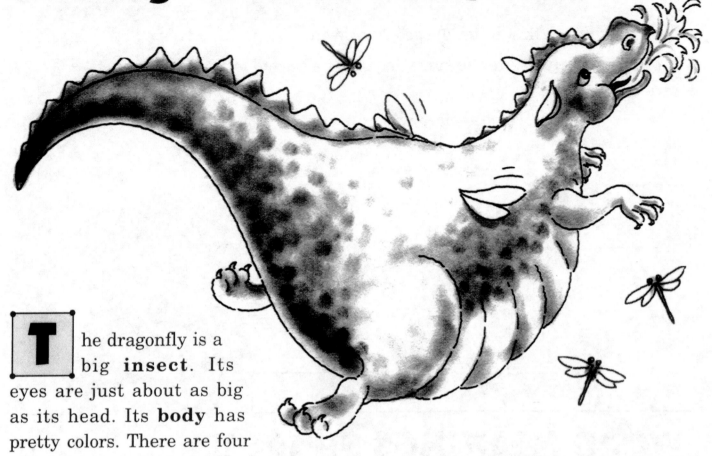

The dragonfly is a big **insect**. Its eyes are just about as big as its head. Its **body** has pretty colors. There are four long **wings** on the body.

Some people are **afraid** of the dragonfly. They may think it does many things that it does not do. It does not sting horses. It does not fight snakes. It does not sting people or stitch up their lips!

A dragonfly is fun to **watch** when you know it will not **harm** you. It flies **straight** ahead, back, up, and down. It seems to be dancing in the air.

A dragonfly eats other, smaller insects. In this way it helps people. Do not be afraid of a dragonfly. Just watch and **enjoy** it.

"The first time I saw it, I couldn't believe my eyes!"

expert exclaims.

UNLOCK THE MYSTERY

What does this story tell last?

Check the best answer.

○ A dragonfly has four wings.

○ People are afraid of dragonflies.

○ A dragonfly has big eyes.

○ Dragonflies help people.

ALPHABET CAN BE YOUR FRIEND

Print the New Words on the lines in ABC order.

☞ Look at the first letter of each New Word.
When the first letters are the same, look at the second letters.

w<u>a</u>sh comes before **w<u>i</u>sh**

SHOO
BUGS!
SHOO!

1. _____

2. _____

3. _____

4. _____

5. _____

6. _____

7. _____

8. _____

WORD MEANINGS SHAPE UP

Use a New Word to finish each meaning. Fill in the word shapes.

1. "Having fear" means ⬚⬚⬚⬚⬚ .

2. To "hurt" means to ⬚⬚⬚⬚ .

3. To "look at" means to ⬚⬚⬚⬚⬚ .

4. "In a line or not curved" means ⬚⬚⬚⬚⬚⬚⬚⬚ .

5. To have fun or get pleasure from is to ⬚⬚⬚⬚⬚ .

6. A bug with six legs is an ⬚⬚⬚⬚⬚⬚ .

7. The main part of an animal is its ⬚⬚⬚⬚ .

8. Things birds and bugs use to fly are ⬚⬚⬚⬚⬚ .

SENTENCES LEFT INCOMPLETE

Finish the sentences.
Print the New Words on the lines.

1. A little animal with six legs is called

   an _____ .

2. Do not be _____ of most insects.

3. Most insects do not _____ people.

4. Animals that fly have _____ .

5. I do not _____ hearing a mosquito fly

   around me.

6. A baby bird has a big head and a little

   _____ .

7. I like to _____ Mom when she is

   working.

8. She showed me how to use a ruler to draw a

   _____ line.

A DRAGONFLY BY ANY OTHER NAME...

Dragonflies are also called "darning needles" because they were once thought to sew people's lips together, or "snake doctors" because they were believed to attack snakes. Even though neither of these beliefs is true, the names still stick.

HOMONYMS MAKE HOLE WHOLE

👉 **Homonyms** are words that sound the same but have different spellings and meanings.

sale and **sail**

Read the letter. Circle the homonyms that make sense in the sentences.

Dear Ashley,

I can hardly [weight, wait] for you [two, to] visit! I [know, no] we will have a great time. We will have [sew, so] much fun! We can spend the [whole, hole] afternoon at the beach! [See, Sea] you soon!

Your friend,

Jenny

FLY...

...TO THE LIBRARY!

Read:

- *Damsels and Dragonflies* by Linda Losito. (Watts, 1988)

- *Dragonflies* by Hidetomo Oda. (Raintree, 1986)

- *Dragonflies* by Barrie Watts. (Silver Burdett Press, 1989)

READERS REVEAL SECRET FEARS!

Some people are afraid of dragonflies. What are you afraid of? Write about something you find scary.

These questions will help you get started:
- What does it look like?
- How does it make you feel?
- Why is it so scary?

Draw your favorite scary thing on another sheet of paper. Then write about it. Use at least three of your New Words.

66

 Now it's time for the test flight!

SECRETS TO SUCCESS ON TESTS

Read all directions carefully. You may even want to read them a second time to make sure you understand.

Read each group of words. Fill in the circle next to the word or words that mean the opposite of the underlined word.

1 enjoy the music
- Ⓐ play
- Ⓑ love
- Ⓒ hate
- Ⓓ listen to

2 harm people
- Ⓐ help
- Ⓑ talk to
- Ⓒ fear
- Ⓓ enjoy

3 afraid of snakes
- Ⓐ fear
- Ⓑ fond
- Ⓒ front
- Ⓓ scared

4 straight line
- Ⓐ stripe
- Ⓑ box
- Ⓒ bent
- Ⓓ even

Read each sentence. Fill in the circle next to the word that best completes the sentence.

5 A fly is a kind of _____.
- Ⓐ insect
- Ⓑ body
- Ⓒ wings
- Ⓓ snake

6 Your arms and legs are parts of your _____.
- Ⓐ boat
- Ⓑ wings
- Ⓒ body
- Ⓓ insect

7 Our windows on the airplane were right over the _____.
- Ⓐ wings
- Ⓑ winter
- Ⓒ walk
- Ⓓ world

8 Amy likes to _____ nature programs on TV.
- Ⓐ watch
- Ⓑ wave
- Ⓒ wind
- Ⓓ wiggle

9 The baby was _____ of the dark.
- Ⓐ wrong
- Ⓑ straight
- Ⓒ afraid
- Ⓓ fair

10 The teacher asked us to make a _____ row.
- Ⓐ sorry
- Ⓑ stray
- Ⓒ straw
- Ⓓ straight

STOP

CORN EXPLODES!
CREATES TASTE SENSATION!

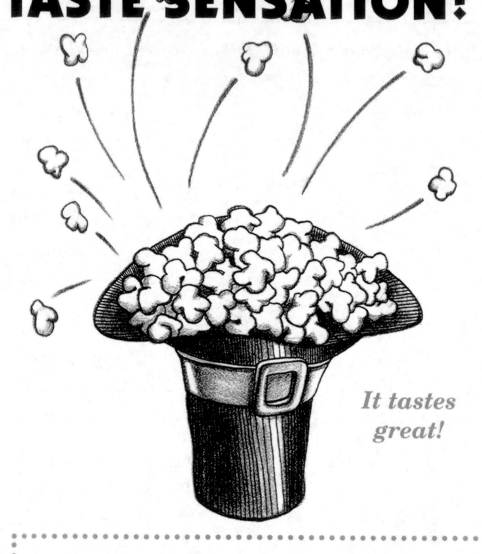

It tastes great!

Did you know that **popcorn** is a **treat** that has been popular for hundreds of years? Some say that on the **first** Thanksgiving Day in 1621 the Native Americans showed the Pilgrims how to cook popcorn.

The corn used to make popcorn has a hard shell. The white part we like to eat is **inside**. Also inside the hard shell is a little water. When the corn is **heated**, the heat changes the water into **steam**. The steam pushes so hard that the shell blows up. It pops! All at once, the white part pops out. It gets much bigger. It almost covers the old shell. The old shell seems to **peek** out of a white cloud.

When you eat popcorn, think of how it pops. Also, **remember** the Native Americans. They discovered this great treat to heat and eat.

STORY EVENTS POP IN ORDER

Which of these things happens first?
Check the best answer.

○ The water changes to steam.

○ The shell blows up.

○ The steam pushes on the shell.

○ The popcorn is heated.

New Words

popcorn

steam

treat

remember

first

peek

heated

inside

Print the New Words on the lines in ABC order.

👉 Look at the first letter of each New Word. When the first letters are the same, look at the second letters.

p<u>e</u>n comes before **p<u>o</u>nd**

1. _____   5. _____

2. _____   6. _____

3. _____   7. _____

4. _____   8. _____

WORD MEANINGS FINALLY BOXED IN

Use a New Word to finish each meaning. Fill in the word shapes.

1. When you look in a secret way, you ☐☐☐☐ .

2. "Made hot" means ☐☐☐☐☐☐ .

3. A food that is fun to eat is a ☐☐☐☐☐ .

4. Very hot water turns into ☐☐☐☐☐ .

Need help? Use the glossary on page 103.

5. "In a thing or within" means ☐☐☐☐☐☐ .

6. The one that comes before all others is ☐☐☐☐☐ .

7. Corn that blows up when heated is ☐☐☐☐☐☐☐ .

8. To "think about again" means ☐☐☐☐☐☐☐☐ .

69

HOLES IN SENTENCES NEED FIXING NOW

Finish the sentences. Print the New Words on the lines.

1. We saw _____ coming up from the hot water.

2. Always _____ to use a potholder to pick up a hot pan.

3. The warm water inside the pot was _____ .

4. Grandpa will _____ into the pot to see what is cooking.

5. One day in school we had a _____ .

6. Jim's mother brought in _____ for everyone.

7. "A" is the _____ letter of the alphabet.

8. We saw a picture that showed the _____ of a palace.

CORNY BUT TRUE

Scientists have found evidence that the corn plant has existed for at least 60,000 years! In earlier days, wild corn on the cob was only three-fourths of an inch long!

New Words

remember	steam	popcorn	heated
first	treat	peek	inside

70

TURN THE PAGE ON POPCORN

After snacking, be sure to read:
- *Corn is Maize: The Gift of the Indians* by Aliki. (HarperCollins, 1976)
- *Corn Belt Harvest* by Bial Raymond. (Houghton Mifflin, 1991)
- *Corn: What It Is, What It Does* by Cynthia Kellogg. (Greenwillow, 1989)

EYEWITNESS BLOWS LID OFF WORD SEARCH CASE!

Circle each New Word in the word search.

```
S C H O E L P L Y
T R E A T M O X S
E S A F P U P H I
A N T P E P C I N
M R E Q E R O L N
B L D T K A R S D
I N S I D E N A A
I N F I R S T R N
X R E M E M B E R
```

FAVORITE FOODS FEARED LOST FOREVER

Some people like popcorn. Which foods do you like?

Here are some questions to think about:
- What does your favorite food taste like?
- Do you remember the first time you ate it?
- Is it easy to prepare the food?

Now pretend that the food you like best is lost. No one in the world can find it. What would you do? Write four or more sentences on another sheet of paper. Use at least three New Words.

Pop over to the test!

SCORE HIGHER ON TESTS

Answer all test questions you're sure of. Don't spend a lot of time on difficult questions. After you have gone through the test once, go back to the questions you skipped.

Read each group of words. Fill in the circle next to the word or words that mean the opposite of the underlined word.

1 remember the number
- Ⓐ count
- Ⓑ find out
- Ⓒ forget
- Ⓓ think about

2 inside the house
- Ⓐ room
- Ⓑ outside
- Ⓒ door
- Ⓓ near

3 heated the water
- Ⓐ cooled
- Ⓑ drank
- Ⓒ warmed
- Ⓓ spilled

4 first in line
- Ⓐ second
- Ⓑ beginning
- Ⓒ last
- Ⓓ nearest

Read each group of words. Fill in the circle next to the word or words that mean the same as the underlined word.

5 peek at the answers
- Ⓐ remember
- Ⓑ read
- Ⓒ write
- Ⓓ look

6 water turned to steam
- Ⓐ steal
- Ⓑ popcorn
- Ⓒ mist
- Ⓓ treat

7 eat popcorn
- Ⓐ kind of food
- Ⓑ hard shell
- Ⓒ fruit
- Ⓓ steam

8 afternoon treat
- Ⓐ wrong
- Ⓑ music
- Ⓒ something to enjoy
- Ⓓ wings

9 heated the air
- Ⓐ cooled
- Ⓑ made hot
- Ⓒ enjoyed
- Ⓓ peeked

10 remember me
- Ⓐ think of
- Ⓑ peek
- Ⓒ inside
- Ⓓ push

72

TODAY'S CHICKENS ARE CHAMPS! ◆

SUPER HENS WON'T STOP LAYING!

Chickens that lay eggs are called **hens**. Years ago, most hens would lay a single egg on one day and then rest on the **next** day. A very good hen would lay 200 eggs in one year.

Farmers wanted their hens to lay more eggs. So they got **busy**. They tried to make hens lay more eggs. They took the eggs from the best **layers**. Baby hens came from those eggs. The babies grew up to lay more eggs than ever.

Farmers kept their hens in henhouses day and night. They fooled the hens by turning on the lights at night. The hens thought more days had **passed**. So they ate more food and laid more eggs.

Hens still do not lay more than one egg each day. **Prize** winners, though, lay more than 300 eggs in a year. (Remember, there are 365 days in a year.) When you eat an egg for **breakfast**, you are eating a hard day's work for a hen!

CHICKEN AND EGG DEBATE CONTINUES

What happened after lights in the henhouse were turned on?

Check the best answer.

◯ The hens ate more.

◯ The hens laid 200 eggs in a year.

◯ The hens rested for a day.

◯ Farmers could find the hens.

THE AMAZING ALPHABET

Print the New Words on the lines in ABC order.

☞ Look at the first letter of each New Word. When the first letters are the same, look at the second letters.

p<u>a</u>n comes before **p<u>r</u>int**

1. _____

2. _____

3. _____

4. _____

5. _____

6. _____

7. _____

8. _____

New Words
layers
breakfast
farmers
prize
hens
busy
passed
next

WORDS AND MEANINGS HATCH TOGETHER!

Use a New Word to finish each meaning. Fill in the word shapes.

1. The first meal of the day is ⬜⬜⬜⬜⬜⬜⬜⬜⬜ .

2. People who work on farms are ⬜⬜⬜⬜⬜⬜⬜ .

3. "Gone by" means ⬜⬜⬜⬜⬜⬜ .

4. The one coming just after is ⬜⬜⬜⬜ .

5. Chickens that lay eggs are called ⬜⬜⬜⬜ .

6. "Having a lot to do" means ⬜⬜⬜⬜ .

7. Something given to a winner is a ⬜⬜⬜⬜⬜ .

8. The farmers kept the eggs from the best ⬜⬜⬜⬜⬜⬜ .

Need help?
Use the
glossary on
page 103.

74

SENTENCES KEEP EGGS IN ONE BASKET

Finish the sentences. Print the New Words on the lines.

1. Jamie liked to eat cereal for _____ .

2. Susie raised _____ for her science project.

3. One of her hens won a _____ .

4. The vacation _____ very quickly.

5. The _____ helped each other pick the fields of corn.

6. The farmer's hens were prize-winning _____ .

7. Carlos will be in the third grade _____ year.

8. The class was too _____ to take a morning break.

BARNYARD POPULARITY CONTEST

The chicken is the most popular farm animal in the history of the world. Maybe that's because, even though it's a bird, it cannot fly away!

CRACK OPEN THESE BOOKS

- *The Easter Egg Farm* by Mary J. Auch. (Holiday House, 1992)
- *Chicken Little* by Beverly C. Burgess. (Harrison House, 1987)
- *Why the Chicken Crossed the Road* by David Macaulay. (Houghton Mifflin, 1987)

WORDS LINK TOGETHER TO FORM GROUP

Each New Word underlined below helps to name a group. Circle the three words that belong in the group.

1. raised by <u>farmers</u>

   chickens   corn   fruit   fill

2. having feathers like <u>hens</u>

   crow   rooster   fruit   duck

3. eaten at <u>breakfast</u>

   eggs   hungry   toast   jam

 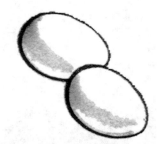  

WHAT IF YOUR HEN RULED THE ROOST?

Look at the picture to the left. Pretend you have raised a prize-winning hen. She laid more than 300 eggs last year! Your teacher asked you to write a news report for your class paper.

These questions will help you get started:
- How did you raise the hen?
- What did you do with the eggs?
- What prizes did she win?

Write your news report on another sheet of paper. Use at least three New Words.

You've gathered your eggs!
Now take the test!

SECRETS TO SUCCESS ON TESTS

Never leave an answer blank. Think about the question and make your very best guess.

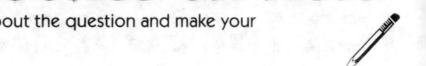

Read each group of words. Fill in the circle next to the word that means the <u>same</u> as the underlined word or words.

1   the <u>one after this one</u>
- Ⓐ neat
- Ⓑ next
- Ⓒ first
- Ⓓ last

2   the <u>chickens that lay eggs</u>
- Ⓐ contests
- Ⓑ farmers
- Ⓒ breakfast
- Ⓓ hens

3   is <u>working hard</u>
- Ⓐ busy
- Ⓑ bunny
- Ⓒ resting
- Ⓓ farmers

4   time <u>went by</u>
- Ⓐ during
- Ⓑ passed
- Ⓒ pushed
- Ⓓ changed

Read each sentence. Fill in the circle next to the word that best completes the sentence.

5   To win an award is to get a _____.
- Ⓐ layer
- Ⓑ pride
- Ⓒ prize
- Ⓓ breakfast

6   You eat _____ in the morning.
- Ⓐ next
- Ⓑ breakfast
- Ⓒ lunch
- Ⓓ treat

7   People who grow food for others are called _____.
- Ⓐ frames
- Ⓑ hens
- Ⓒ farmers
- Ⓓ layers

8   We will do it on the _____ sunny day.
- Ⓐ past
- Ⓑ busy
- Ⓒ passed
- Ⓓ next

9   Hens called _____ make the eggs we eat.
- Ⓐ farmers
- Ⓑ layers
- Ⓒ players
- Ⓓ chickens

10   Dad was _____ making breakfast.
- Ⓐ afraid
- Ⓑ passed
- Ⓒ next
- Ⓓ busy

PONCE DE LEÓN SEARCHES FOR THE FOUNTAIN OF YOUTH

READERS ASK, WHY?

Why did Ponce de León name the land he discovered "Florida"?

Check the best answer.

- ☐ The land had no fountain.
- ☐ It was a sunny land.
- ☐ It was a place where many flowers grew.
- ☐ Many people lived there.

What would happen if your **grandparents** could take a bath in magic water? Then, in a **moment**, they became your age! Long ago there was a man named Ponce de León who believed he could find such a magic bath. He had heard about a **fountain** in a far-away place. Its water was supposed to make people **young**. He thought the story might be true.

Ponce de León went to look for this fountain. Instead, he found a **sunny** land. The land was filled with flowers. He named the land *Florida*. That means "land of flowers."

Ponce de León **visited** Florida two times but never did **discover** the "Fountain of Youth." Today many people go to Florida. They do not discover the "Fountain of Youth" either. But they do find a **lovely** land filled with flowers and sunshine.

ALPHABET KEEPS NEW WORDS YOUNG

Print the New Words on the lines in ABC order.

1. _____

2. _____

3. _____

4. _____

5. _____

6. _____

7. _____

8. _____

NEW WORDS

• • • • • •

grandparents
young
lovely
sunny
fountain
moment
discover
visited

Words Find Meaning in Life

★ ★ ★ ★ ★ ★ ★ ★

Use a New Word to finish each meaning. Fill in the word shapes.

1. "Being in the first part of life, or not old," means ⬜⬜⬜⬜⬜.

2. "Went to stay with" means ⬜⬜⬜⬜⬜⬜⬜.

3. "Beautiful or good looking" means ⬜⬜⬜⬜⬜⬜.

4. A place from which water comes is a ⬜⬜⬜⬜⬜⬜⬜⬜.

5. To find for the first time is to ⬜⬜⬜⬜⬜⬜⬜⬜.

6. A short bit of time is a ⬜⬜⬜⬜⬜⬜.

7. The mother and father of a child's mother and father are ⬜⬜⬜⬜⬜⬜⬜⬜⬜⬜⬜⬜.

8. The sky on a clear day is ⬜⬜⬜⬜⬜.

MISSING WORDS COMPLETE SENTENCES!

Finish the sentences. Print the New Words on the lines.

1. The parents of your mother and father are called

   your _____ .

2. I got a cool drink from that _____ .

3. Last week I went to the country and _____

   my grandmother.

4. It takes just a _____ to write your name.

5. The buds on the plant became _____

   flowers.

6. I always wear sunglasses on a _____ day.

7. Did you _____ the prize in the box?

8. Jack was too _____ to drive a car.

NEW WORDS

moment

lovely

grandparents

fountain

sunny

young

visited

discover

FOUNTAIN OF KNOWLEDGE DISCOVERED!

Stay young. Read these books:

- *Ponce de León* by Wyatt Blassingame.
  (Chelsea House, 1991)

- *Panther Glade* by Helen Cavanagh.
  (Simon and Schuster, 1991)

- *The Missing 'Gator of Gumbo Limbo:*
  An Ecological Mystery by Jean C. George.
  (Harper Collins, 1992)

WAS PONCE DE LEÓN RIGHT?

Ponce de León began his search for the fountain of youth on the island of Bimini in the Bahamas. Modern scientists have found a mineral spring there that they believe may really have healing powers!

ACROSS

Use the New Words to finish the puzzle.

2. went to see
6. mother and father of a child's mother and father
7. not old
8. a very short time

DOWN

1. bright and shining
3. to find
4. water flows from here
5. beautiful

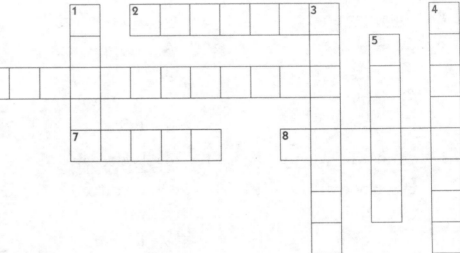

MYSTERY MANSION

OLD HOUSE HOLDS MANY SECRETS

 Look at the picture. Imagine that you and your friends find an old house. No one lives there. What should you do? What happens next?

Use these questions to help tell about the old house:

- What do your friends do?
- Do you hear any strange sounds?
- What animals or people do you discover there?

Now write a letter to your grandparents on another sheet of paper. Tell them all about the house. Use at least three New Words.

Discover the test on the next page!

IMPROVE YOUR SCORE

Look at all possible answers. Skip the ones that you are sure are incorrect. Decide which of the remaining answers is best.

Read each group of words. Fill in the circle next to the word or words that mean the _opposite_ of the underlined word.

1 <u>discover</u> gold
- Ⓐ find
- Ⓑ lose
- Ⓒ enter
- Ⓓ use

2 <u>sunny</u> day
- Ⓐ cloudy
- Ⓑ bright
- Ⓒ warm
- Ⓓ hot

3 <u>visited</u> the family
- Ⓐ stopped by
- Ⓑ called on
- Ⓒ went to
- Ⓓ left

4 <u>lovely</u> dress
- Ⓐ beautiful
- Ⓑ nice
- Ⓒ long
- Ⓓ ugly

5 feel <u>young</u>
- Ⓐ bad
- Ⓑ strong
- Ⓒ old
- Ⓓ sad

Read each sentence. Fill in the circle next to the word or words that best complete the definition.

6 A <u>fountain</u> is a—
- Ⓐ family
- Ⓑ house
- Ⓒ pen
- Ⓓ pool of water

7 <u>Grandparents</u> are the parents of your—
- Ⓐ young
- Ⓑ parents
- Ⓒ old
- Ⓓ Florida

8 A <u>moment</u> is another name for a—
- Ⓐ mother
- Ⓑ fountain
- Ⓒ long time
- Ⓓ bit of time

9 To <u>discover</u> is to—
- Ⓐ find
- Ⓑ lose
- Ⓒ swim
- Ⓓ read

10 <u>Visited</u> means
- Ⓐ passed
- Ⓑ went to see
- Ⓒ discovered
- Ⓓ danced

BALLERINA POPS WHEELIES AT NUTCRACKER PERFORMANCE

"**W**ho made up the **rule** that you have to dance on your own two feet?" asks Mary Verdi Fletcher. Mary Verdi Fletcher doesn't let the fact that she can't walk stop her. Mary dances from her wheelchair. She dips and turns just like any **dancer**. But **unlike** other dancers, she even pops a few wheelies!

When Mary was a young girl, her grandmother told her, "Mary, your **disability** is a gift. You must use it to deliver a message." Today Mary believes that anyone can **express** himself or herself through dance.

Mary helped **found** a new dance **troupe** called Dancing Wheels. Some of the dancers in the troupe can use their feet, and others **perform** from wheelchairs. In her wheelchair Mary glides with the ease and grace of a skater. She is breaking new ground for dancers all over the world.

"Popping wheelies is not only fun, it's an art form," says Mary.

CAUSE IS REVEALED

Why does Mary Fletcher dance in a wheelchair?

Check the best answer.

- ◯ Mary can go faster in the wheelchair.
- ◯ Mary has a disability.
- ◯ Mary is learning to dance.
- ◯ Mary wants to be like other dancers.

THE ALPHABET DANCE

Write the New Words in aphabetical order.

☞ Look at the first letter of each New Word. When the first letters are the same, use the second letters.

d<u>a</u>rk comes before **d<u>i</u>nner**

New Words

rule
dancer
unlike
disability
express
found
troupe
perform

1. _____

2. _____

3. _____

4. _____

5. _____

6. _____

7. _____

8. _____

WORDS DEFINED

Use a New Word to finish each meaning. Fill in the word shapes.

1. Something that guides the way a person behaves is called a ⬚⬚⬚⬚.

2. A group of dancers, singers, or other performers is a ⬚⬚⬚⬚⬚⬚.

3. To put into words or actions is to ⬚⬚⬚⬚⬚⬚⬚.

4. Something different from is ⬚⬚⬚⬚⬚⬚.

5. To start something is to ⬚⬚⬚⬚⬚.

6. Anything that limits a person's ability to do something is a ⬚⬚⬚⬚⬚⬚⬚⬚⬚⬚.

7. A person who moves the body to music is a ⬚⬚⬚⬚⬚⬚.

8. To act or dance for other people is to ⬚⬚⬚⬚⬚⬚⬚.

84

DANCE AROUND THESE SENTENCES

Write the New Word that best completes each sentence.

1. The dance _____ performed for the school.

2. It is hard for me to _____ myself in words.

3. My broken leg is a _____ for me.

4. We are going to _____ our play for your class.

5. My parents want to _____ a new kind of organization.

6. The _____ moved across the stage.

7. I am _____ my sister when it comes to sports.

8. The _____ is that you must be home by 6:00 P.M.

DO WHEELIES THROUGH THESE SCRAMBLES

Unscramble the New Words and write them on the lines.

New Words

rule express
dancer found
unlike troupe
disability perform

1. dfuon _____

2. eurl _____

3. oprteu _____

4. froperm _____

5. klineu _____

6. xspeesr _____

7. nraecd _____

8. bytiasdili _____

READ:

- "The Most Able Among Us." (*KidSports Magazine*, May/June, 1993)
- *If You Were a Ballet Dancer* by Ruth Belov Gross. (Dial Press, 1979)

WATCH:

- *Nutcracker — The Motion Picture.* (Goodtimes, 1986)
- *The Nutcracker* or *Swan Lake* at your local ballet.

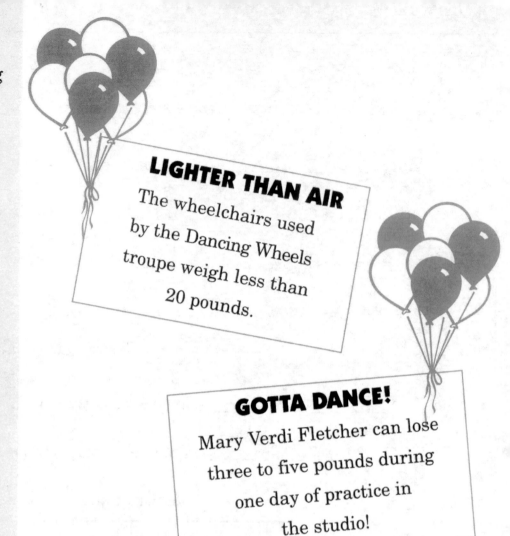

LIGHTER THAN AIR

The wheelchairs used by the Dancing Wheels troupe weigh less than 20 pounds.

GOTTA DANCE!

Mary Verdi Fletcher can lose three to five pounds during one day of practice in the studio!

THE GREATEST SHOW ON EARTH

What if you could go to see Mary's troupe perform? What do you think the show would be like? Write a story about what you might see.

These questions will help you get started:
- What is the show about?
- In what ways is this show the same or different from others you have seen?
- What is the best part of the show?

Use three of the New Words in your story.

Get your wheels rolling and take the test!

TEST-DAY TIPS TOLD

Look for hints in the words to help you understand the meaning of the underlined word.

Read each group of words. Fill in the circle next to the word or words that mean the same as the underlined word.

1 <u>perform</u> on ice
- Ⓐ see a show
- Ⓑ do an act
- Ⓒ hear
- Ⓓ wheel

2 <u>unlike</u> her brother
- Ⓐ along with
- Ⓑ next to
- Ⓒ the same as
- Ⓓ different from

3 follow the <u>rule</u>
- Ⓐ law
- Ⓑ game
- Ⓒ dance
- Ⓓ wheel

4 dance <u>troupe</u>
- Ⓐ group
- Ⓑ family
- Ⓒ school
- Ⓓ building

Read each sentence. Fill in the circle next to the word that best completes the sentence.

5 The ____ moved across the stage.
- Ⓐ disability
- Ⓑ dare
- Ⓒ dancer
- Ⓓ dark

6 Mary did not let her ____ stop her.
- Ⓐ dancer
- Ⓑ rule
- Ⓒ troupe
- Ⓓ disability

7 It is sometimes hard to ____ the way you feel.
- Ⓐ found
- Ⓑ express
- Ⓒ perform
- Ⓓ enter

8 She plans to ____ a school to help the blind.
- Ⓐ give
- Ⓑ rule
- Ⓒ express
- Ⓓ found

9 The actors ____ in the play.
- Ⓐ express
- Ⓑ found
- Ⓒ perform
- Ⓓ rule

10 Do you know the ____ about returning books?
- Ⓐ rule
- Ⓑ troupe
- Ⓒ books
- Ⓓ dancers

CAMELS HAVE THREE EYELIDS
FOUR-LEGGED DUNE BUGGY HAS MANY EXTRAS!

Camels are made for hot, **dry** lands. They can go without food or water for days. They keep food in the form of fat in their humps. They can smell water from miles away.

Camels have **padded** feet with two large toes. Their feet are good for walking on the **soft** sands of the desert.

The eyes, noses, and ears of camels are also made for dry lands. The stinging, blowing sand does not hurt them **badly**. Camels have three **eyelids**. One is under the other two. This eyelid is **clear**, and a camel can see **while** it is closed. On the **outer** eyelids, camels have thick eyelashes. Thick hairs in their noses and ears also help them keep out the blowing sand. Camels are built to stand up to the harsh climate they face every day.

"Hey friend, need a lift?"

CLOSE CHECK SHOWS CLEAR CAUSE

Why are a camel's eyes not hurt by the blowing sand?

Check the best answer.

◯ There is no sand where they live.

◯ Camels have three eyelids.

◯ Camels have hairs in their noses.

◯ Camels have padded feet.

New Words

padded

outer

dry

while

soft

eyelids

badly

clear

THE AMAZING ALPHABET

Print the New Words on the lines in ABC order.

1. _____   5. _____

2. _____   6. _____

3. _____   7. _____

4. _____   8. _____

WORDS AND MEANINGS REUNITED

Finish each meaning, using a New Word from the box. Fill in each word shape.

1. "Not hard" means ⬜⬜⬜⬜ .

2. Folds of skin that go over the eye are ⬜⬜⬜⬜⬜⬜ .

3. Something that can be seen through is ⬜⬜⬜⬜⬜ .

4. "At the same time" means ⬜⬜⬜⬜⬜ .

5. "Stuffed with something soft" means ⬜⬜⬜⬜⬜⬜ .

6. "On the side that is out" means ⬜⬜⬜⬜⬜ .

7. "Very much or not well" means ⬜⬜⬜⬜⬜ .

8. "Not wet" means ⬜⬜⬜ .

Need help?
Use the
glossary on
page 103.

WORDS DESERT SENTENCES

New Words

- eyelids
- dry
- soft
- padded
- clear
- while
- outer
- badly

Finish the sentences. Print a New Word on each line.

1. During the race Mark wanted some water
   _____.

2. He wanted the water becuse his mouth was very
   _____.

3. The box was _____ with newspaper so
   that the glass inside would not break.

4. The _____ covering was made of plastic.

5. We waited _____ Mary called her Mom
   on the phone.

6. Your _____ close when you blink or go to
   sleep.

7. The window was _____ after we
   washed it.

8. Dad thinks a _____ pillow is better than
   a hard pillow.

ONE HUMP OR TWO?

- There are two kinds of camels. The Arabian camel has one hump.
  The Bactrian camel has two.

- Camels chew their cud like cows. Cows and camels have several
  stomachs. Before their food passes from one to another, it comes back
  up to be chewed some more! Yuck!

LEARN AT HOME IN YOUR SPARE TIME

Read more about camels:

- *Camels* by Donna Bailey. (Raintree, 1992)

- *Camels* by John Nexo. (Creative Education, 1989)

- *Pamela Camel* by Bill Peet. (Houghton Mifflin, 1986)

READERS TELL OF STRANGE ANIMALS

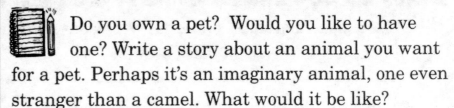

Do you own a pet? Would you like to have one? Write a story about an animal you want for a pet. Perhaps it's an imaginary animal, one even stranger than a camel. What would it be like?

These questions will help you get started:
- What does the animal look like?
- How do you play with it?
- What is the animal called?

Now write three or more sentences on another sheet of paper. Tell about your pet. Then draw a picture of it. Use at least three New Words.

ARE SYNONYMS SIMILAR OR ALIKE?

YOU BE THE JUDGE!

👉 **Synonyms** are words with nearly the same meaning.

big and **large**

fast and **swift**

Pick words from the Synonym Tree.

Draw lines to the baskets with the right synonyms.

WHILE

SOFT

DRY

LOVELY

SMALL

tiny   when   thirsty   fluffy   pretty

91

TEST-TAKING SECRETS REVEALED

If you make a mistake, erase the wrong answer entirely. Don't forget to mark the correct answer for that question.

Look at each picture. Fill in the circle next to the word that best fits the picture.

1

Ⓐ badly
Ⓑ eyelid
Ⓒ clear
Ⓓ padded

2

Ⓐ salt
Ⓑ soft
Ⓒ safe
Ⓓ some

3

Ⓐ padded
Ⓑ page
Ⓒ clear
Ⓓ while

Read each sentence. Fill in the circle next to the word that best completes the sentence.

4 If you can see through the glass, it is _____.

Ⓐ soft
Ⓑ cheer
Ⓒ clear
Ⓓ dry

5 The part on the outside is the _____ part.

Ⓐ other
Ⓑ only
Ⓒ under
Ⓓ outer

6 Some people have funny dreams _____ they are sleeping.

Ⓐ what
Ⓑ while
Ⓒ why
Ⓓ which

7 A desert is very _____.

Ⓐ dry
Ⓑ dark
Ⓒ clean
Ⓓ clear

8 We lost the game because we played _____

Ⓐ padded
Ⓑ dry
Ⓒ badly
Ⓓ outer

9 You can see far on a _____ day.

Ⓐ padded
Ⓑ soft
Ⓒ dry
Ⓓ clear

10 The camel uses its _____ feet to walk in the sand.

Ⓐ dry
Ⓑ soft
Ⓒ padded
Ⓓ outer

FRANKLIN MAKES *SHOCKING* DISCOVERY!
MYSTERY FORCE CHANGES WORLD FOREVER

Long ago, people knew little about **electricity**. They thought it was magic. Benjamin Franklin knew it was not magic. He was one of the first people to learn about electricity. His friends liked to see him do tricks with it. He made their **hair** stand on end. The electricity **felt** funny. It made them jump. Their **puzzled** looks made others laugh.

Working with electricity was not a **joke** to Franklin. He found out new things about it. Once he flew a kite in a **storm**. The kite went up to the **lightning** in the clouds. The string got wet. Franklin could feel electricity. He got a small **shock**.

Since Benjamin Franklin, many others have learned much about electricity. Today its magic is all around us.

A HAIR-RAISING EXPERIENCE

What made people's hair stand on end?

Check the best answer.

○ storms

○ magic

○ lightning

○ electricity

ELECTRIC
ALPHABET

New Words

electricity

joke

shock

storm

felt

hair

puzzled

lightning

Print the New Words on the lines in ABC order.

☞ Look at the first letter of each New Word. When the first letters are the same, look at the second letters.

short comes before **st**ill

1. _____   5. _____

2. _____   6. _____

3. _____   7. _____

4. _____   8. _____

WORDS AND MEANINGS MATCH . . . AND THAT'S NO JOKE!

Use a New Word to finish each meaning. Fill in the word shapes.

1. A type of power that can move along a wire is ☐☐☐☐☐☐☐☐☐☐☐ .

2. "Surprised or mixed up" means ☐☐☐☐☐☐☐ .

3. A flash of light in the sky is ☐☐☐☐☐☐☐☐☐ .

4. "Touched or knew about by touching" means ☐☐☐☐ .

5. What grows out of people's heads is ☐☐☐☐ .

6. A funny story or trick is a ☐☐☐☐ .

7. A sudden pain or unhappy surprise is a ☐☐☐☐☐ .

8. A strong wind with rain or snow is a ☐☐☐☐☐ .

Ahead of His Time!

Ben Franklin's last public act before his death in 1790 was to sign a petition asking for an end to slavery.

EXPERT COMPLETES SENTENCES...

...WITH LIGHTNING SPEED!

Finish the sentences. Print the New Words on the lines.

1. _____ flashed across the sky.

2. If you go outside in the rain without a hat, your _____ will get wet.

3. The _____ had strong winds.

4. The children laughed when the teacher told a funny _____ .

5. Have you ever _____ the soft fur of a cat?

6. I am _____ by this problem.

7. The toaster uses _____ .

8. Be careful not to get a _____ .

READ ALL ABOUT IT

Check out these great books:

- *What's the Big Idea, Ben Franklin?* by Jean Fritz. (Putnam, 1982)

- *Ben & Me* by Robert Lawson. (Little Brown, 1988)

- *Ben Franklin's Glass Armonica* by Bryna Stevens. (Dell, 1992)

HEART STARTS WITH A

The human body depends on electricity. About every second a small electric signal triggers the heart to beat.

WORD SEARCH CLOUDS THE ISSUE
SOLUTION EXPECTED SOON

Circle the New Words in the word search.

New Words

```
E C F E E J O K P H A
C S H O C K S E O E P
P S B J O K E R Y M U
R T U E Z L E D H B Z
M O Y F T Q R O A S Z
V R N R M K I A I N L
E M C F E L T G R D E
D L I G H T N I N G D
E L E C T R I C I T Y
```

hair

lightning

joke

puzzled

electricity

felt

storm

shock

Stormy Weather Ahead

Think of the worst storm you have ever been in. Write a story about what happened.

These questions will help you get started:
- What did you see and hear?
- Where were you?
- How did you feel?

Write your story on another sheet of paper.
Use at least three New Words.

The storm has cleared. Take the test!

SCORE HIGHER ON TESTS

If you have time at the end of a test, reread the directions and test questions to see if you made any careless mistakes.

Look at each picture. Fill in the circle next to the word that best fits the picture.

1.
   - Ⓐ puzzled
   - Ⓑ shock
   - Ⓒ storm
   - Ⓓ felt

2.
   - Ⓐ like
   - Ⓑ light
   - Ⓒ dark
   - Ⓓ lightning

3.
   - Ⓐ hare
   - Ⓑ hear
   - Ⓒ hair
   - Ⓓ here

4.
   - Ⓐ felt
   - Ⓑ joke
   - Ⓒ puzzled
   - Ⓓ story

Read each sentence. Fill in the circle next to the word or words that best complete the sentence.

5. The power to run a TV is . . . .
   - Ⓐ storm
   - Ⓑ lightning
   - Ⓒ electricity
   - Ⓓ felt

6. A funny story is a. . . .
   - Ⓐ joke
   - Ⓑ puzzle
   - Ⓒ storm
   - Ⓓ shock

7. To get a jolt is to get a . . . .
   - Ⓐ felt
   - Ⓑ shock
   - Ⓒ lightning
   - Ⓓ joke

8. To be confused is to be . . . .
   - Ⓐ puzzled
   - Ⓑ padded
   - Ⓒ joined
   - Ⓓ shocked

9. If you touched a rabbit's fur, you might say it . . . .
   - Ⓐ hopped fast
   - Ⓑ felt soft
   - Ⓒ sat still
   - Ⓓ seemed happy

10. Strong wind and heavy rain are called a . . . .
    - Ⓐ lightning
    - Ⓑ shock
    - Ⓒ heat
    - Ⓓ storm

YOGURT STARTS NEW FOOD CRAZE

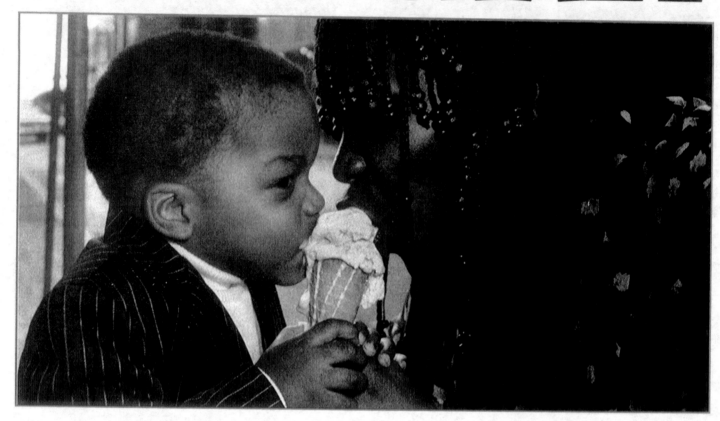

Long ago, a thirsty traveler crossed the desert. He opened his goatskin bag to have a sip of milk. But tiny living cells called **bacteria** had changed his cool liquid to a thick custard. And it had a **taste** that was **sour**! Was the man's milk spoiled? No. He had a bag of **yogurt**!

Two kinds of bacteria are added to milk to make yogurt. These "good" bacteria change liquid milk to a thick, **creamy curd**. Some people like this **dairy** treat flavored with fruit or juice. Frozen yogurt is a popular treat that has less fat than ice cream. Yogurt is a **healthful** food people love. Who knows? Little Miss Muffet's curds may have been plain or flavored yogurt!

ZERO IN ON YOGURT

What is this story mainly about?

Check the best answer.

- ❑ how to make yogurt
- ❑ who first made yogurt
- ❑ kinds of yogurt
- ❑ all about yogurt

THE A, B, C'S OF YOGURT

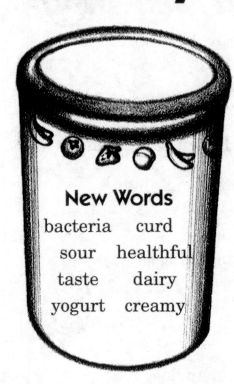

New Words

bacteria   curd
sour   healthful
taste   dairy
yogurt   creamy

Write the New Words in alphabetical order.

☞Look at the first letter of each New Word. When the first letters are the same, use the second letters.

crook comes before **cu**t

1. _____   5. _____

2. _____   6. _____

3. _____   7. _____

4. _____   8. _____

WORDS AND MEANINGS MATCH

Use a New Word to finish each meaning. Fill in the word shapes.

1. A word that describes products made from milk is ⬚⬚⬚⬚⬚ .

2. "Flavor" means almost the same as ⬚⬚⬚⬚⬚ .

3. When milk thickens it forms a ⬚⬚⬚⬚ .

4. The little cells that help make yogurt are ⬚⬚⬚⬚⬚⬚⬚⬚ .

5. Foods that are good for you are ⬚⬚⬚⬚⬚⬚⬚⬚⬚ .

6. If you keep milk too long, it will turn ⬚⬚⬚⬚ .

7. When yogurt is smooth, we say it is ⬚⬚⬚⬚⬚⬚ .

8. A dairy food often flavored with fruit or juice is ⬚⬚⬚⬚⬚⬚ .

SENTENCED TO A YOGURT DIET

WORDS HELP TO COMPLETE SENTENCES

Write the New Word that best completes each sentence.

New Words

bacteria
sour
taste
yogurt
creamy
curd
dairy
healthful

1. There was a _____ frosting on the cake.

2. Some _____ are good for you, and some are bad.

3. Vegetables are part of a _____ diet.

4. The milk tastes _____ .

5. I like small _____ cottage cheese.

6. Cheese is a _____ food.

7. I like strawberries in my _____ .

8. Do you like the _____ of apples?

WORD MIX-UP IS PUZZLING

Circle each New Word in the word search.

F	W	D	B	C	S	K	T	S
V	B	C	R	E	A	M	Y	O
E	A	H	U	T	J	G	Y	U
X	C	L	Q	A	R	J	O	R
D	T	Y	C	S	Z	I	G	K
H	E	A	L	T	H	F	U	L
A	R	E	P	E	C	U	R	D
M	I	H	G	I	B	O	T	A
F	A	N	D	A	I	R	Y	L

WHAT'S FOR SUPPER?

 Some people like yogurt, and others would rather eat meat or vegetables. What is your favorite food? Write about it.

These questions will help you get started:

- What do you get to eat on your birthday?
- When you go to the store, what kinds of food do you like to buy?
- What food smells the best to you?

Use three of the New Words as you write about your favorite food.

READING CAN BE HEALTHFUL

READ:

- *Future Food.* (Crestwood House, 1980)

- *What's on Your Plate?* by Noral Smaridge. (Abingdon, 1982)

- *The Wonderful World of Yogurt* by Dorothy Parker. (Hawthorn Books, 1972)

- *Frozen Yogurt* by Mable Hoffman. (Fisher Books, 1990)

SCOOP UP THE FACTS

You can make yogurt at home. Just add a teaspoon of plain yogurt to some milk and leave it in a warm spot. But take care! Move the yogurt as little as possible. The living bacteria don't like to be disturbed when they're growing!

Cows drink as much as twenty gallons of water every day.

IMPROVE YOUR SCORE

Read all directions carefully. You may even want to read them a second time to make sure you understand them.

Read each group of words. Fill in the circle next to the word or words that mean the _same_ as the underlined word.

1 ate some <u>curd</u>
- Ⓐ meat
- Ⓑ candy
- Ⓒ ice cream
- Ⓓ thickened milk

2 liked the <u>taste</u>
- Ⓐ sound
- Ⓑ flavor
- Ⓒ looks
- Ⓓ feel

3 <u>healthful</u> foods
- Ⓐ spoiled
- Ⓑ bad
- Ⓒ favorite
- Ⓓ good

4 good <u>bacteria</u>
- Ⓐ cells
- Ⓑ insects
- Ⓒ germs
- Ⓓ people

Read each sentence. Fill in the circle next to the word that best completes the sentence.

5 She used the ____ milk to bake a cake.
- Ⓐ flavor
- Ⓑ sour
- Ⓒ used
- Ⓓ sound

6 I like strawberries in my ____ .
- Ⓐ yogurt
- Ⓑ meat
- Ⓒ potatoes
- Ⓓ noodles

7 Ice cream and yogurt are ____ foods.
- Ⓐ bad
- Ⓑ bacteria
- Ⓒ dairy
- Ⓓ curd

8 I stirred the cake batter until it was ____ .
- Ⓐ healthful
- Ⓑ sour
- Ⓒ curd
- Ⓓ creamy

9 He likes the ____ of fruit.
- Ⓐ sound
- Ⓑ taste
- Ⓒ curd
- Ⓓ bacteria

10 Some ____ are good for us.
- Ⓐ fights
- Ⓑ trees
- Ⓒ germ
- Ⓓ bacteria

GLOSSARY

Pronunciation Key

Letters	Show the Sound of	Written as
a	cat	KAT
ah	odd	AHD
ahr	bar	BAHR
aw	lawn	LAWN
ay	pay	PAY
b	bib	BIB
ch	chip	CHIP
d	deed	DEED
e	pet	PET
ee	bee	BEE
er	care	KER
eye	island	EYE luhnd
f	fast	FAST
g	gag	GAG
h	hat	HAT
i	pit	PIT
ir	dear	DIR
j	joke	JOHK
k	kit	KIT
l	lid	LID
m	man	MAN
n	no	NOH
ng	thing	THING
oh	go	GOH
oo	moon	MOON
or	store	STOR
ow	out	OWT
oy	joy	JOY
p	pop	PAHP
r	rat	RAT
s	see	SEE
sh	ship	SHIP
t	tin	TIN
th	thing	THING
th	then	THEN
u	book	BUK
uh	cut	KUHT
ur	her	HUR
v	vase	VAYS
w	with	WITH
y	yet	YET
z	zebra	ZEE bruh
zh	vision	VIZH uhn

A a

ac•tor (AK tor) *n.* a person who plays a part in a movie

add•ed (AD uhd) *v.* were put with others

a•fraid (ah FRAYD) *adj.* having fear

al•most (AWL mohst) *adv.* nearly

an•tics (AN tiks) *n.* playful or silly actions

ap•pears (uh PIRZ) *v.* comes into sight

ar•my (AHR mee) *n.* a group that fights in a war

a•round (ah ROWND) *prep.* in many parts of

B b

bad•ly (BAD lee) *adv.* very much; not well

bac•te•ri•a (bak TIR ee ah) *n.* little cells that help make yogurt

bal•let (ba LAY) *n.* a kind of graceful dance

ba•nan•a (buh NAN uh) *n.* a ripe fruit with yellow skin

base•ball (BAYS bawl) *n.* a game played with a bat and ball

beach (BEECH) *n.* the sandy edge of a lake

beau•ti•ful (BYOO ti fuhl) *adj.* pretty

bod•y (BAHD ee) *n.* the main part of an animal

break•fast (BREK fahst) *n.* the first meal of the day

bub•bles (BUHB uhlz) *n.* balls of air

build•ings (BILD ingz) *n.* structures such as houses and schools

bunch (BUHNCH) *n.* a group of things in one place together

bus•y (BIZ ee) *adj.* having a lot to do

C c

cen•ter (SEN ter) *n.* middle

clear (KLIR) *adj.* able to be seen through

co•coa (KOH koh) *n.* a sweet, brown, hot drink

cos•tumes (KAHS toomz) *n.* special clothes, such as those that mascots wear

coun•try (KUHN tree) *n.* a land where people live

cream•y (KREEM ee) *adj.* smooth

curd (KURD) *n.* thickened milk

D d

dair•y (DER ee) *adj.* a word that describes products made from milk

dance (DANS) *v.* to move to music

danc•er (DAN ser) *n.* a person who moves the body to music

deep•er (DEEP er) *adv.* down more and more

de•scribe (di SKREYEB) *v.* to tell what something is like

dic•tion•ar•y (DIK shuh ner ee) *n.* a book of words and their meanings

dis•a•bil•i•ty (dis uh BIL i tee) *n.* anything that limits a person's ability to do something

dis•cov•er (di SKUHV er) *v.* to find for the first time

doz•ens (DUHZ enz) *n.* things that are in groups of twelve

dream (DREEM) *n.* an idea or hope for a better life

dry (DREYE) *adj.* not wet

E e

e•lec•tric•i•ty (ee lek TRIS i tee) *n.* a type of power that can move along a wire

en•joy (en JOY) *v.* to have fun or get pleasure from

ev•er•y (EV ree) *adj.* each one

ev•er•y•thing (EV ree thing) *pron.* all things

ex•plor•ers (ek SPLOR erz) *n.* people who go to new places

ex•press (eks PRES) *v.* to put into words or actions

eye•lids (EYE lidz) *n.* folds of skin that go over the eye

F f

fair (FER) *adj.* the same for everyone

farm•ers (FAHR merz) *n.* people who work on farms

felt (FELT) *v.* touched or knew about by touching

first (FURST) *adj.* coming before all others

fla•vor (FLAY ver) *n.* taste

flow•er (FLOW er) *n.* the part of the plant that grows from the bud

fought (FAWT) *v.* had a fight

found (FOWND) *v.* to start something

foun•tain (FOWNT uhn) *n.* a place from which water comes

free•dom (FREE duhm) *n.* the state of being able to choose what you want to do

front (FRUHNT) *n.* the part that is not in the back

fruit (FROOT) *n.* part of a plant that can taste good

fur•ry (FUR ee) *adj.* soft and hairy

G g

game (GAYM) *n.* a sport or contest

gen•i•us (JEEN yuhs) *n.* a very smart person

grand•par•ents (GRAND per uhnts) *n.* the mother and father of a child's mother and father

guest (GEST) *n.* a person who comes to visit

H h

hair (HER) *n.* what grows out of people's heads

harm (HAHRM) *v.* to hurt

health•ful (HELTH fuhl) *adj.* good for you

heat•ed (HEET ed) *v.* made hot

heav•y (HEV ee) *adj.* hard to lift

hens (HENZ) *n.* chickens that lay eggs

holes (HOHLZ) *n.* things you can dig in the ground

hun•gry (HUNG gree) *adj.* needing or wanting food

I i

in•sect (IN sekt) *n.* a bug with six legs

in•side (in SEYED) *adv.* in a thing; within

J j

joke (JOHK) *n.* a funny story or trick

jump•ing (JUMP ing) *v.* leaping

K k

king•dom (KING duhm) *n.* a land ruled by a king

L l

lat•er (LAYT er) *adv.* after a time

laws (LAWZ) *n.* rules that tell what people can do

lay (LAY) *v.* to put out eggs

lay•ers (LAY erz) *n.* hens that lay eggs

light•ning (LEYET ning) *n.* a flash of light in the sky

love•ly (LUHV lee) *adj.* beautiful; good looking

lurks (LURKS) *v.* lies in wait

M m

mar•ket (MAHR kuht) *n.* a place where things are sold

mas•cot (MAS kaht) *n.* a team's good-luck pet

mat•ter (MAT er) *v.* to make a difference

mo•ment (MOH muhnt) *n.* a short bit of time

mouth (MOWTH) *n.* the part of your body through which you take in food

mov•ies (MOOV eez) *n.* shows put on film

N n

near•by (nir BEYE) *adj.* near

next (NEKST) *adj.* the one coming just after

nurs•er•y (NURS er ee) *n.* a room for little children

o o

o•pen (OH puhn) *adj.* not shut

out•er (OWT er) *adj.* on the side that is out

P p

pad•ded (PAD uhd) *adj.* stuffed with something soft

passed (PASD) *v.* gone by

peek (PEEK) *v.* to look in a secret way

peo•ple (PEE puhl) *pl. n.* men, women, and children

per•form (per FORM) *v.* to act or dance for other people

plac•es (PLAYS ez) *n.* spaces where things are

plant (PLANT) *n.* a living thing such as a bush

play•ers (PLAY urz) *n.* people who take part in games

po•ems (POH uhmz) *n.* verses such as nursery rhymes

poor (POR) *adj.* having very little

pop•corn (PAHP korn) *n.* corn that blows up when heated

prac•tice (PRAK tis) *v.* to do something over and over

pret•ty (PRIT ee) *adj.* something that is pleasant to look at

print•ed (PRINT ed) *v.* made into a book

prize (PREYEZ) *n.* something given to a winner

puz•zled (PUHZ uhld) *adj.* surprised or mixed up

R r

re•mem•ber (ree MEM ber) *v.* to think about again

rhymes (REYEMZ) *n.* poems that use words with the same end sounds

ripe (REYEP) *adj.* ready to pick and use for food

robs (RAHBZ) *v.* takes from others

rule (ROOL) *n.* something that guides the way a person behaves

S s

sea (SEE) *n.* a large body of salt water

shells (SHELZ) *n.* the soft or hard coverings of eggs

shock (SHAHK) *n.* a sudden pain or unhappy surprise

sil•ly (SIL ee) *adj.* foolish

skills (SKILZ) *n.* abilities

slide (SLEYED) *v.* to move along smoothly

small (SMAWL) *adj.* little

smell (SMEL) *v.* to have an odor

soft (SAWFT) *adj.* not hard

sol•diers (SOHL jerz) *n.* people in the army

sour (SOWR) *adj.* spoiled

speak (SPEEK) *v.* to say something

spo•ken (SPOH kuhn) *v.* said

stage (STAYJ) *n.* a raised platform

steam (STEEM) *n.* the misty state of very hot water

sticks (STIKS) *v.* reaches or extends out

stick•y (STIK ee) *adj.* holding to other things like glue

storm (STORM) *n.* a strong wind with rain or snow

straight (STRAYT) *adj.* in a line; not curved

strong (STRONG) *adj.* full of power, or mighty

sun•ny (SUHN ee) *adj.* having sunlight like the sky on a clear day

T t

tails (TAYLZ) *n.* the parts on the ends of animals

taste (TAYST) *n.* flavor

team (TEEM) *n.* people who work or play together as a group

thank•ful (THANK fuhl) *adj.* feeling thanks

them•selves (them SELVZ) *pron.* their own or true selves

through (THROO) *prep.* from the beginning to the end of

tongue (TUHNG) *n.* the muscle in your mouth

tore (TOR) *v.* ripped or took apart

trained (TRAYND) *v.* showed how to or taught

treat (TREET) *n.* a food that is fun to eat

troupe (TROOP) *n.* a group of dancers, singers, or other performers

U u

ug•ly (UHG lee) *adj.* not at all pretty

un•like (un LEYEK) *prep.* different from

V v

vis•it•ed (VIZ it ed) *v.* went to stay with

vote (VOHT) *v.* to choose or to say whom you want to win

W w

watch (WAHCH) *v.* to look at

while (HWEYEL) *conj.* at the same time

wig•gle (WIG uhl) *v.* to go back and forth

wings (WINGZ) *n.* things birds and bugs use to fly

win•ter (WIN ter) *n.* a cold time of year

world (WURLD) *n.* our earth

wrong (RONG) *adj.* not right

Y y

yo•gurt (YOH gert) *n.* a dairy food often flavored with fruit or juice

young (YUHNG) *adj.* being in the first part of life; not old

Answer Key

Fish Dance on the Beach
pages 3-7

Latest Details on Dancing Fish
It lays its eggs.

Alphabet Keeps Words in Line
1. beach
2. dance
3. deeper
4. holes
5. lay
6. sea
7. tails
8. wiggle

Words and Meanings Together Again
1. lay
2. deeper
3. wiggle
4. beach
5. holes
6. sea
7. tails
8. dance

Incomplete Sentences Found in Book
1. beach
2. holes
3. deeper
4. sea
5. tails
6. dance
7. wiggle
8. lay

Words Join Together to Form New Groups
1. sand, shells, water
2. snake, worm, tooth
3. fish, seaweed, ships

Test-taking Secrets Revealed
1. A
2. C
3. B
4. D
5. C
6. A
7. B
8. D
9. C
10. B

Ballet for Fun and Fitness
pages 8-12

Check Those Details
to join a dance team

Jump into the Alphabet
1. ballet
2. game
3. jumping
4. players
5. practice
6. pretty
7. skills
8. stage

Today's Match: Words and Meanings
1. jumping
2. players
3. pretty
4. stage
5. skills
6. game
7. ballet
8. practice

Athletes Fill in the Blanks
1. ballet
2. stage
3. practice
4. jumping
5. pretty
6. skills
7. game
8. players

Free the Hidden Words

```
C P B E Q Y J B V
P R A C T I C E B
L E L O A D X Z T
A T L I G A M E F
Y T E L E P R K D
E Y T S K I L L S
R F S T A G E S E
S G N A M W A G U
H J U M P I N G C
```

Test-day Tips Told
1. D
2. B
3. A
4. B
5. D
6. C
7. A
8. C
9. D
10. C

Children Speak Dozens of Languages
pages 13-17

Find the Detail
the Bantu language of Africa

Alphabet Orders New Words
1. around
2. buildings
3. describe
4. dictionary
5. dozens
6. explorers
7. speak
8. spoken

Mystery Solved: Words Match Meanings
1. buildings
2. speak
3. dictionary
4. around
5. explorers
6. dozens
7. spoken
8. describe

Words Plug Sentence Holes
1. buildings
2. around
3. explorers
4. describe
5. dictionary
6. spoken
7. dozens
8. speak

Sounds Alone Are Not the Answer
1. d
2. c
3. b
4. a
5. f
6. h
7. e
8. g
9. eye
10. I
11. so
12. sew

Improve Your Score
1. B
2. C
3. A
4. D
5. A
6. C
7. B
8. D
9. A
10. D

Washington Leads Winter Warriors
pages 18-22

Details, Attention!
go home

Alphabet Army on the March
1. army
2. country
3. hungry
4. people
5. soldiers
6. through
7. trained
8. winter

Word Match Hits the Target
1. people
2. army
3. winter
4. trained
5. country
6. hungry
7. soldiers
8. through

Missing Words Surrounded
1. winter
2. country
3. army
4. soldiers
5. people
6. hungry
7. trained
8. through

Scrambled Words Hide Secret Message
soldiers
through
winter
trained
hungry
people
country

Score Higher on Tests
1. C
2. D
3. A
4. C
5. B
6. C
7. D
8. D
9. B
10. B

Shoppers Go Bananas!
pages 23-27

Details Can Get Under Your Skin
about 150

Alphabet Tree Sprouts New Words
1. banana
2. bunch
3. every
4. flavor
5. fruit
6. market
7. plant
8. ripe

Words and Meanings Match
1. every
2. ripe
3. market
4. plant
5. fruit
6. banana
7. flavor
8. bunch

Completed Sentences Bear Fruit
1. fruit
2. banana
3. flavor
4. bunch
5. every
6. ripe
7. plant
8. market

Top Banana Solves Fruit Riddle
1. bananas
2. market
3. flavor
4. plant
5. red
Answer to riddle: salad

Secrets to Success on Tests
1. D
2. B
3. C
4. B
5. D
6. D
7. A
8. C
9. A
10. B

It's a Bird! It's a Moose! It's a Mascot!
pages 28-32

Mascots Have the Right Idea
baseball mascots

Alphabet Keeps Words in Order
1. baseball
2. costumes
3. furry
4. mascot
5. silly
6. slide
7. team
8. tongue

Words Cheer for Meanings
1. slide
2. mascot
3. team
4. baseball
5. silly
6. costumes
7. furry
8. tongue

New Words Complete Sentences
1. slide
2. costumes
3. mascot
4. baseball
5. team
6. tongue
7. furry
8. silly

Secret to Analogies Revealed
1. silly
2. team
3. baseball
4. furry

Test-taking Secrets Revealed
1. B
2. A
3. D
4. B
5. B
6. D
7. C
8. D
9. D
10. A

Mother Goose Found!
pages 33-37

Story Holds Key to Main Idea
how some rhymes came to be

The Amazing Alphabet
1. added
2. almost
3. nursery
4. places
5. poems
6. printed
7. rhymes
8. small

Hidden Meanings Can Be Found
1. almost
2. places
3. nursery
4. rhymes
5. printed
6. small
7. poems
8. added

Cure Found for Incomplete Sentences!
1. nursery
2. poems
3. rhymes
4. printed
5. almost
6. small
7. places
8. added

Puzzler
Across
1. nursery
4. poems
6. almost
7. added

Down
2. rhymes
3. printed
4. places
5. small

Test-day Tips Told
1. A
2. C
3. D
4. A
5. D
6. B
7. C
8. C
9. A
10. B

Snake's Eggs Ready to Crack!
pages 38-42

Story Hatches Main Idea
"The Eggs of Snakes"

Alphabet Can't Be Beat
1. bubbles
2. everything
3. front
4. mouth
5. open
6. shells
7. sticks
8. themselves

Which Came First, the Meaning or the Word?
1. everything
2. bubbles
3. shells
4. open
5. mouth
6. front
7. themselves
8. sticks

Frogs Leap at Chance to Complete Sentences
1. shells
2. themselves
3. front
4. mouth
5. open
6. sticks
7. everything
8. bubbles

Antonym Puzzle Finally Solved
1. nothing
2. closed
3. rear
4. others

Secrets to Success on Tests
1. B
2. C
3. B
4. C
5. B
6. A
7. D
8. B
9. C
10. D

Ancient Aztec Kingdom Once Ruled Mexico
pages 43-47

Exciting Main Idea Found in Aztec Story!
a strong group of people

New Words Show Alphabetical Order
1. beautiful
2. center
3. cocoa
4. fought
5. kingdom
6. later
7. strong
8. tore

New Words Match Old Meanings
1. cocoa
2. beautiful
3. strong
4. later
5. center
6. fought
7. kingdom
8. tore

Words Needed to Fill Sentence Holes
1. cocoa
2. later
3. beautiful
4. strong
5. center
6. tore
7. kingdom
8. fought

Words of a Feather Group Together
1. land, people, king
2. talking, running, playing
3. chair, rug, table

Improve Your Score
1. D
2. C
3. A
4. C
5. B
6. D
7. B
8. C
9. B
10. D

Nerd Alert!
pages 48-52

Main Idea Found in Story
Jaleel White

Think Alphabetically
1. actor
2. antics
3. appears
4. genius
5. guest
6. lurks
7. movies
8. nearby

Help Find Word Meanings
1. antics
2. nearby
3. appears
4. movies
5. lurks
6. actor
7. guest
8. genius

Words Fill Sentence Holes
1. actor
2. antics
3. movies
4. guest
5. nearby
6. genius
7. appears
8. lurks

Free the Hidden Words

```
A Y B A N T I C S
O A X C D J M Z P
J P N T B H P L G
W P M O V I E S U
N E A R B Y A G E
Q A C V C E R K S
D R E L U R K S T
H S G E N I U S F
G I T K P S U M O
```

Score Higher on Tests
1. D
2. B
3. A
4. C
5. B
6. C
7. A
8. D
9. D
10. C

Flower Power
pages 53-57

Order Found in Flower Story
the size of the flower

Alphabet Makes Words Grow!
1. flower
2. heavy
3. robs
4. smell
5. sticky
6. thankful
7. ugly
8. world

Connection Found Between Words and Meanings!
1. world
2. heavy
3. smell
4. sticky
5. thankful
6. flower
7. ugly
8. robs

Missing Words Cause Sentence Holes
1. ugly
2. smell
3. heavy
4. world
5. thankful
6. flower
7. sticky
8. robs

Things You Never Knew About . . . Antonyms
1. e
2. c
3. a
4. b
5. d
6. c
7. e
8. a
9. d
10. b

Test-taking Secrets Revealed
1. D
2. C
3. B
4. A
5. D
6. B
7. C
8. C
9. A
10. B

"I Have a Dream!"
pages 58-62

Life Story Has Meaning
Dr. Martin Luther King, Jr., helped get laws changed.

Alphabetical Order
1. dream
2. fair
3. freedom
4. laws
5. matter
6. poor
7. vote
8. wrong

Connection Found Between Words and Meanings
1. laws
2. vote
3. wrong
4. poor
5. matter
6. freedom
7. fair
8. dream

Word Expert Fills Sentence Holes!
1. poor
2. fair
3. freedom
4. laws
5. vote
6. matter
7. wrong
8. dream

Puzzling Evidence

Across
3. wrong
4. vote
5. freedom
7. matter

Down
1. dream
2. poor
5. fair
6. laws

Test-day Tips Told
1. B
2. D
3. C
4. B
5. D
6. B
7. A
8. D
9. C
10. A

Have You Ever Seen a Dragon Fly?
pages 63-67

Unlock the Mystery
Dragonflies help people.

Alphabet Can Be Your Friend
1. afraid
2. body
3. enjoy
4. harm
5. insect
6. straight
7. watch
8. wings

Word Meanings Shape Up
1. afraid
2. harm
3. watch
4. straight
5. enjoy
6. insect
7. body
8. wings

Sentences Left Incomplete
1. insect
2. afraid
3. harm
4. wings
5. enjoy
6. body
7. watch
8. straight

Homonyms Make Hole Whole
wait
to
know
so
whole
See

Secrets to Success on Tests
1. C
2. A
3. B
4. C
5. A
6. C
7. A
8. A
9. C
10. D

Today's Chickens Are Champs!
pages 73-77

Chicken and Egg Debate Continues
The hens ate more.

The Amazing Alphabet
1. breakfast
2. busy
3. farmers
4. hens
5. layers
6. next
7. passed
8. prize

Words and Meanings Hatch Together!
1. breakfast
2. farmers
3. passed
4. next
5. hens
6. busy
7. prize
8. layers

Sentences Keep Eggs in One Basket
1. breakfast
2. hens
3. prize
4. passed
5. farmers
6. layers
7. next
8. busy

Words Link Together to Form Group
1. chickens, corn, fruit
2. crow, rooster, duck
3. eggs, toast, jam

Secrets to Success on Tests
1. B
2. D
3. A
4. B
5. C
6. B
7. C
8. D
9. B
10. D

Corn Explodes!
pages 68-72

Story Events Pop in Order
The popcorn is heated.

More Amazing Alphabet
1. first
2. heated
3. inside
4. peek
5. popcorn
6. remember
7. steam
8. treat

Word Meanings Finally Boxed In
1. peek
2. heated
3. treat
4. steam
5. inside
6. first
7. popcorn
8. remember

Holes in Sentences Need Fixing Now
1. steam
2. remember
3. heated
4. peek
5. treat
6. popcorn
7. first
8. inside

Eyewitness Blows Lid off Word Search Case!

```
S C H O E L P L Y
T R E A T M O X S
E S A F P U P H I
A N T P E P C I N
M R E Q E R O L N
B L D T K A R S D
I N S I D E N A A
I N F I R S T R N
X R E M E M B E R
```

Score Higher on Tests
1. C
2. B
3. A
4. C
5. D
6. C
7. A
8. C
9. B
10. A

Ponce de León Searches for the Fountain of Youth
pages 78-82

Readers Ask, Why?
It was a place where many flowers grew.

Alphabet Keeps New Words Young
1. discover
2. fountain
3. grandparents
4. lovely
5. moment
6. sunny
7. visited
8. young

Words Find Meaning in Life
1. young
2. visited
3. lovely
4. fountain
5. discover
6. moment
7. grandparents
8. sunny

Missing Words Complete Sentences!
1. grandparents
2. fountain
3. visited
4. moment
5. lovely
6. sunny
7. discover
8. young

Puzzle Page
Across
2. visited
6. grandparents
7. young
8. moment

Down
1. sunny
3. discover
4. fountain
5. lovely

Improve Your Score
1. B
2. A
3. D
4. D
5. C
6. D
7. B
8. D
9. A
10. B

Ballerina Pops Wheelies at Nutcracker Performance
pages 83-87

Cause Is Revealed
Mary has a disability.

The Alphabet Dance
1. dancer
2. disability
3. express
4. found
5. perform
6. rule
7. troupe
8. unlike

Words Defined
1. rule
2. troupe
3. express
4. unlike
5. found
6. disability
7. dancer
8. perform

Dance Around These Sentences
1. troupe
2. express
3. disability
4. perform
5. found
6. dancer
7. unlike
8. rule

Do Wheelies Through These Scrambles
1. found
2. rule
3. troupe
4. perform
5. unlike
6. express
7. dancer
8. disability

Test-day Tips Told
1. B
2. D
3. A
4. A
5. C
6. D
7. B
8. D
9. C
10. A

Camels Have Three Eyelids
pages 88-92

Close Check Shows Clear Cause
Camels have three eyelids.

The Amazing Alphabet
1. badly
2. clear
3. dry
4. eyelids
5. outer
6. padded
7. soft
8. while

Words and Meanings Reunited
1. soft
2. eyelids
3. clear
4. while
5. padded
6. outer
7. badly
8. dry

Words Desert Sentences
1. badly
2. dry
3. padded
4. outer
5. while
6. eyelids
7. clear
8. soft

Are Synonyms Similar or Alike?
soft—fluffy
small—tiny
while—when
dry—thirsty
lovely—pretty

Test-taking Secrets Revealed
1. B
2. B
3. A
4. C
5. D
6. B
7. A
8. C
9. D
10. C

Franklin Makes Shocking Discovery!
pages 93-97

A Hair-raising Experience
electricity

Electric Alphabet
1. electricity
2. felt
3. hair
4. joke
5. lightning
6. puzzled
7. shock
8. storm

Words and Meanings Match . . . and That's No Joke!
1. electricity
2. puzzled
3. lightning
4. felt
5. hair
6. joke
7. shock
8. storm

Expert Completes Sentences . . . with Lightning Speed!
1. Lightning
2. hair
3. storm
4. joke
5. felt
6. puzzled
7. electricity
8. shock

Word Search Clouds the Issue

```
E C F E E J O K P H A
C S H O C K S E O E P
P S B J O K E R Y M U
R T U E Z L E D H B Z
M O Y F T Q R O A S Z
V R N R M K I A I N L
E M C F E L T G R D E
D L I G H T N I N G D
E L E C T R I C I T Y
```

Score Higher on Tests
1. C
2. D
3. C
4. B
5. C
6. A
7. B
8. A
9. B
10. D

Yogurt Starts New Food Craze
pages 98-102

Zero in on Yogurt
all about yogurt

The A, B, C's of Yogurt
1. bacteria
2. creamy
3. curd
4. dairy
5. healthful
6. sour
7. taste
8. yogurt

Words and Meanings Match
1. dairy
2. taste
3. curd
4. bacteria
5. healthful
6. sour
7. creamy
8. yogurt

Sentenced to a Yogurt Diet
1. creamy
2. bacteria
3. healthful
4. sour
5. curd
6. dairy
7. yogurt
8. taste

Word Mix-up Is Puzzling

```
F W D B C S K T S
V B C R E A M Y O
E A H U T J G Y U
X C L Q A R J O R
D T Y C S Z I G K
H E A L T H F U L
A R E P E C U R D
M I H G I B O T A
F A N D A I R Y L
```

Improve Your Score
1. D
2. B
3. D
4. A
5. B
6. A
7. C
8. D
9. B
10. D